The Story and Science of Preventing Conflict
and Creating Lifetime Love

emotional
**connection**

DR. MICHAEL & PAULA REGIER

MichaelRegier.com

# Table of Contents

---

part one

## BROKEN PROMISES: *Blindsided by Betrayal*

---

part two

## TRAUMA: *Face-to-Face with Our Enemies*

---

part three

## EARLY CHILDHOOD:
### *How Parents Shape Childhood Attachment*

# Acknowledgments

What you will read between the covers of this book is a labor of many hours, hands and hearts. We owe thanks to so many whose encouragement, feedback and teaching have allowed us to stay on this journey in order to get this message out to couples across the globe.

First and foremost, we, Michael and Paula, are grateful to each other. We wanted a book that would represent both of our voices. Writing together in this creative fiction/nonfiction format has been rewarding and challenging. We so appreciate the encouraging words that kept us in a process of finding a fresh way to reach the hearts of our readers.

Thank you to Ken Petersen, writer, editor and friend. We are forever grateful for your coaching, developmental editing, and writing. And more so for your shared passion for this life-giving message of attachment. This work would not have found its legs without you.

Thank you to Christopher Orr for your brilliant cover design. To our copy editor, Laura Ross, for objectivity that made the manuscript more clear and accessible. And thanks to Katherine Lloyd for your careful and creative interior book design. Julia Loren, Blue Moth Media, thanks for encouraging us very early in our journey. Your introduction to the folks at Baker Books facilitated our finding the help we needed to launch this project.

We are privileged to have been students of some of the finest leaders in the field of Emotionally Focused Therapy and Attachment Theory. This has formed the foundation for the book. Thank you Dr. Sue Johnson for developing the EFT model and for your skillful teaching. A personal thank you to Dr. Rebecca Jorgensen for your technical training in Emotionally Focused Therapy and to Dr. Lisa Palmer-Olsen who was invaluable in helping Michael through the EFT certification process. Gordon Meredith, Drs. Nancy and Paul Aikin, Matt Angelstorf and Murray Armstrong, thanks so much for your training and support.

Thank you to all of our clients who have trusted us with your love relationships, your most intimate injuries, needs and desires. You have been great examples of repairing and growing attachment bonds and have taught us so much.

Thank you to our family and friends who have believed in us over the years. Marc and Cindy, your support and endurance has been super-human. Thanks to all who have attended our seminars, read our blogs, and have continued to ask for more.

# Introduction

All couples want their marriages to succeed. Yet, most couples have little understanding about what to do to protect and deepen lifetime love. As a result, many marriages appear to succeed on the surface but gradually erode in connection until a crisis threatens to destroy the relationship.

Over time, without a sustained focus on building intimate connection, a marriage becomes dissatisfying to one or both partners. Even the most committed marriages will ultimately fail. For so many, the initial love attraction and even the commitment to stay married are not enough to protect the relationship from disconnection and devastation.

Most husbands and wives find themselves acting out a script that was written long before the two of them even met. They need help to understand how the emotional injuries they brought to the relationship will eventually play themselves out with the other person.

Couples also need to understand what mature love looks like. Mature love is secure love. It looks and feels very different from the exciting attraction of new love. Understanding how to grow and nurture secure love is vital to lifelong relationship success. Most of us have few models of mature adult, securely attached, lifelong love relationships.

This should come as no surprise; it's only in recent years that the theory and science of secure loving attachment have been taught to counselors and therapists. The simple things I communicated in these first few paragraphs haven't always been known.

I will never forget sitting in a room with 250 other therapists as some of these insights were presented to me for the first time by Dr. Sue Johnson, the co-developer of *Emotionally Focused Couples Therapy*. Tears welled in my eyes as I realized the truth of what was being said. I was not alone. When I looked around the room, many around me were teary-eyed, too.

Making love last is not difficult when you know what makes it grow. Every one of us comes into this world wired to connect. We just need to know how to create the connection. Today, there are thousands of well-researched articles discussing how bonds of love are created and nurtured. How to become rich in love is no longer a mystery. The principles in this book will work for you and the people you love. Paula and I are excited to share with you these principles in a creative format we think you will enjoy.

We use three powerful methods to impart the vital keys to a long and fulfilling love relationship: Story, Therapy, and Analysis.

**Story:** We present a singular, compelling story of a couple who thought they had an ideal relationship, yet found themselves in marital crisis. We have created "Ben" and "Claire" as composites of the relationship histories of many couples I see in therapy. Their problems are common, and you will probably see a lot of yourself, or people you know, in their struggle. Their lives are surface-perfect, ideal in a way that many might envy. Slowly and quietly, their honeymoon love slips away and they are blindsided by love's silent killer. Disconnection opens the door to a devastating affair that rips at their marriage foundations. Fortunately, Ben and Claire find professional help and begin to understand the principles of attachment and gain insight into true connection.

The story starts with the crisis that brought Ben and Claire into therapy. What you learn along with them is that what they thought was the problem was only part of it. In most cases, a particular relationship crisis is related to a lifetime of relationship insecurity.

We want readers to understand the big picture of what threatens and what creates lasting love. The story of Ben and Claire begins in the present day and then travels back to their childhood, adolescent, and young-adult relationships. We conclude with a chapter about how they forgive, heal, and create a new life together.

**Therapy:** You may wonder what therapy is like. Here is your chance to have a bird's-eye view of it, through Ben and Claire's weekly therapy sessions. You will be exposed to the emotional battle zone that many couples experience behind the closed doors of the therapist's office. You will see and identify with our characters. You'll witness their feelings of childlike fear and incompetence when their relationship fails. You will experience the danger and devastation of the loss of lifetime love relationships. Therapy for most couples will move more slowly than we portray in this book. The progress that Ben and Claire make in just a few sessions is likely to be made over the course of months of therapy.

**Analysis:** The principles in this book are supported by research. Even if science is not your strong suit, we believe this will resonate for you. For the reader who wants to dig deeper, we provide notes and references that support the science behind the therapy. It's helpful to understand the big picture of what may be contributing to your relationship's success or failure. We share with you the scientifically proven methods that we now use day-in and day-out to help couples see the real enemy lurking within their relationship. Once you, like them, have seen that true enemy, you will have at your fingertips the tools to strengthen and repair your relationship.

This book is for all couples and singles who want to know what makes lifetime love work. We sincerely hope your marriage is not at the critical stage Ben and Claire find themselves in, but, by examining a marriage in crisis, you may be able to avert such a crisis yourself. Understanding what makes love grow and last should bring you the relationship you have longed for.

Yes, some marriages *are* in the fire, much as Ben and Claire's was. If that applies to you, perhaps this book will provide a window into the kind of therapy that can, even now, save you from divorce.

And for those of you who are single, in new relationships, or engaged to be married—those not yet dealing with marital conflict—there is much in these pages of immense value as you embark on your lives together.

We hope our words will be read by clergy, counselors, and caregivers as well, and will shape the advice they give to couples struggling in their relationships. This is foundational truth, we believe, that represents a major shift in how we understand healthy relationship. We invite others to open up to its value.

Ben and Claire were at the edge of a cliff when their marriage blew up. We hope their story and the teachings in this book will help you safeguard your relationship and avoid the emotional trauma of a destroyed relationship. We believe there is nothing more important than making your life partnership loving for a lifetime. To that end, we thank you for joining us in this most exciting of all journeys to achieve that goal!

Michael and Paula Regier

part one
# broken promises

## Blindsided by Betrayal

STORY

# The Heartbreak of Betrayal

*I don't know why they call it heartbreak.*
*It feels like every other part of my body is broken too.*
–Author Unknown

Claire was jolted from a deep sleep as the phone's annoying tweet faded into the room's solitude. *Who's texting at this ridiculous hour?* she wondered, noticing the cold, rumpled sheets that had hours earlier outlined her now-absent husband. She ignored the phone and burrowed into the soft down to ward off the morning's familiar threat of depression. She would not allow loneliness to steal this day. Closing her eyes and taking a breath, she focused on memories of long ago. She recalled the magic of twelve years past. Claire cherished that peaceful, vivid day she had met Ben. . . .

*The buzz of the college quad stilled as Ben hastily made his way toward her. Claire posed against the light pole, trying to disguise her anticipation. Ben saw the concrete bench in his path—but just a split second too late. He scurried to collect his papers before they got caught by the breeze.*

*Claire giggled and bit her lip, watching the endearing sight play out. Ben wished he could redo his grand entrance, but no such luck! Instead, he swallowed hard, despising the taste of his pride. Quickly recovering, he bowed for effect and propelled himself toward Claire.*

Claire soaked in the memory. Her smart and handsome Ben had swept her off her feet. They had embraced life, running toward everything it held for them. They were the perfect couple, compatible and rarely arguing. They meticulously carved out their future . . . together. *Partners for life!* Those had been the three sweetest words of their vows.

Claire squinted in the morning sunlight, drenching herself in the memory of their honeymoon. Though Ben had anticipated Claire's "yes," he'd sweetened his marriage proposal with carefully thought-out honeymoon plans. Claire, and their beginnings as husband and wife, would be well worth the price tag on a month abroad. Med school would be grueling, after all. He would borrow for the honeymoon if need be. Spain, France, Italy . . . what an incredible backdrop for romance, adventure, and amazing photo ops!

*Yes, yes, a thousand times yes. Of course she'd marry Ben.*

*Breathtaking white sand beaches in the south of France...gondola cruises through the canals of Venice...and Spain, with its rich and vibrant culture. The honeymoon was all they'd hoped it would be and more. After long and full days, the newlyweds collapsed onto each other with ravenous passion. Their lovemaking felt as exotic as the countries they found themselves in. Claire adored her husband, but had to admit that she dreaded the abrupt awakening as they catapulted back into the real world. Surreal memories would be their springboard for the next leg of their journey as husband and wife.*

*Back home, Ben and Claire celebrated their love and life in their sparsely appointed Chicago home, popping the cork on cheap bubbly, nervous yet excited to delve into the arduous journey of Ben's medical school and residency.*

Claire hugged her comforter as those perfect memories trans-formed her perspective for the day. A joyful tear wet her face. Claire knew that kids and careers had taken priority over her rela-tionship with Ben, but well...that's just life. Ten years later, she could still dream.

She reached for her phone to silence the persistent message alerts—only to see its blank screen. It wasn't her phone but Ben's that had been vibrating on the nightstand. He must have forgotten it. She fumbled with the device to quiet it, just as it vibrated again, and the words of a text scrolled across the screen.

*Probably shouldn't read it,* she thought. But just before stuffing the phone under the pillow, the texted words came into focus.

*Oh my god.*

Claire's mouth fell open when she saw what was glowing from the small screen—the unfamiliar sender's name and the words that person had typed. Her hands trembled. She frantically tried to make sense of what she was seeing. There it was. Incriminating evidence.

*Who the hell are you, Bridgette, and what are you doing with* . . . Claire couldn't finish—she was struggling for breath.

Ben's morning had been hectic. Patients demanded more of him than he had hours in the day. He took a swallow of cold coffee and grabbed for his cell. It wasn't there. A small stab of panic worked its way down his spine as he emptied his pockets of keys, coins, even lint. His face drained of color as he scanned his desk. Ben knew Bridgette's penchant for sending early morning messages. What if Claire saw one?

He dialed Bridgette's number from his desk phone. Her sultry morning voice went flat when he told her about his oversight. Had she written to him that morning? What, exactly, had she said? He sank in his chair as she recited the contents of her messages. These words would not easily be explained. Ben's life would never be the same and he knew it.

Claire lay motionless, clutching the phone. Time stood still yet raced. *Ben's been at work a few hours. Has he even missed his phone?*

She rushed to the bathroom and soaked her face in cold water. *No, this cannot be happening.* She wandered aimlessly from the bathroom to the closet to the bed…eventually just sinking down onto the floor.

*Oh my god, what do I do?*

Snapping to her senses, Claire threw herself into the task of getting the kids ready for school. Occasionally, the morning routine went off without a hiccup, and she desperately needed it to be that kind of morning.

Dressed, fed, and kissed goodbye at their appropriate drop-off points, the kids saw it as just another day, unaware that Claire had been mechanically going through the motions, her thoughts a million miles away. Once the kids were out of sight, she slipped carefully out of the parking lot, found a quiet spot to pull over, and lost it.

*Oh my gosh, what do I do?*

Claire couldn't go home. She couldn't be there when Ben came in to retrieve his phone. She needed to figure things out first. She needed a plan. Claire dialed her sister, her best friend. Choking back the lump in her throat, she said, "Steph, I have to talk to you. Can you meet me? It's urgent."

Claire met her sister in the parking lot of an abandoned church. She had once captured on film the beauty of its bell tower's weakened mortar against a morning sky. As she stared up at it now, she was overcome with sadness. Her artistic vision crumbled in the grip of her broken spirit.

Claire slumped into the seat next to Steph and began to unspool the story of finding the text messages. As she talked, anger and rage replaced sadness. Then fear. And with that, the tears returned in torrents.

"Steph, you can't imagine the messages. I scrolled backwards and there were dozens of them. They were so intimate . . . kind of steamy, Steph. It was like reading a romance novel." Claire sobbed between words. "They talked like Ben and I used to, years ago—like teenagers in love. It's been forever since he's said those things to me, or even felt them, probably."

Ben sat silenced by fear, calculating his next steps. Racing home to retrieve the phone would mean confrontation, unless of course Claire hadn't discovered the messages. Should he just go ahead and confess his friendship with Bridgette? Their relationship was innocent enough. Friendly colleagues. They hadn't crossed any sexual boundaries.

Ben felt conflicted as he contemplated ending it with Bridgette. She had brought new perspective and energy to him over the past months. Bridgette made Ben feel whole again. He felt understood and appreciated. What would life be like without her?

Ben managed to clear his calendar for the next hour. He clumsily locked the office door and drove home to face the music. But maybe not. *Perhaps she hasn't even seen the messages.*

Claire and Steph talked through options as Claire fought past her anger, hurt, and confusion. She found herself paralyzed by the overwhelming fear of losing her husband. "What if he chooses *her*, Steph?"

The horrifying thought hung in the air. Claire went on: "Maybe I should just ignore all this, never let on that I saw the texts. I can't lose him, Steph. I can't become a divorce statistic. I just—"

"Claire!" Stephanie interrupted. "Slow down. Is that the kind of life you want, burying this and hoping for the best? Is that even living?"

Auntie Steph offered to pick the kids up after school. They could have a sleepover at her place. The cousins loved hanging out, and Claire would need time with Ben to hash things out.

Driving home, Claire still wasn't sure what to do. Her sister's words echoed in her mind. Although grateful for Steph's unconditional love and encouragement, Claire remained just as hurt, confused, and torn as before.

As she pulled up to the house, she was startled at the sight of Ben's car in the driveway. Tentatively, she entered the kitchen, then stopped short at the sight of Ben with his phone in his hand, wearing a deer-in-the-headlights stare. Claire's sadness and uncertainty quickly fell away. Anger and rage shot through her like lightning. She wanted Ben to hurt just as she had been hurt. *He deserves to feel my pain.*

"How dare you cheat on me," she said, her voice trembling. "How dare you have an affair! These texts . . ." Her voice trailed off then came back, wailing, "I hate you Ben, I hate you." She raised her hand and slapped him across the face.

Ben stood shell-shocked. Tears filled his eyes as he saw how deeply he'd hurt his wife. "It's not an affair, Claire," he said, his voice breaking. "We're just friends. I'm really sorry. I didn't mean to hurt you...I'd never want to do that." He paused, wiped a tear from his cheek, and continued. "Trust me, this is not what you're thinking. It's not the big deal you're imagining."

"Not a big deal! You don't think being unfaithful to me is a big deal?"

"I, well, I just . . . It's just not what it seems, Claire."

"It *seems* that you are sexting with another woman, Ben," Claire hissed. "And who knows what else? It's *exactly* what it seems."

Ben hated being in this place. He hated that his emotions were getting the better of him, that he couldn't hold them back. He had to get out. "Please, Claire, I have patients in twenty minutes," he muttered. "I'm swamped with work and have to get back. Could we please talk about this tonight? I'm sure you'll feel better by then."

Claire shook her head in disbelief. "You've gotta get back to the office? That's all you have to say? You coward. You think you can stuff all those intimate texts away in your pocket, and just walk out of here?"

Claire cursed Ben as he left, slamming the door behind him. She lunged for the sink to empty her sour stomach, rinsed her mouth straight from the tap, then stood motionless and watched her tears hit the porcelain. Claire planted her exhausted body in the living room and sat for hours. The lifestyle Claire had dreamed about looked nothing like this.

Claire grabbed her laptop and began searching through a sea of online resources, along with a host of promises for relationship fixes. She landed on Emotionally Focused Therapy, which seemed solid, well supported by research and successful outcomes. Eventually Claire made the call for help.

At six p.m., Ben quietly dropped his bag and coat in the foyer. He couldn't be late. *And if I'm early, Claire may read that as a sort of admission.* Ben had squeezed in another call to Bridgette before leaving his office. It may have been their last, but then again . . . Ben's thoughts swirled in a mess of confusion.

Ben and Claire sat in silence for an eternity. He realized she wasn't going to make this easy. He stuttered through his thoroughly rehearsed explanation, giving just enough detail to appease his wife—or so he thought.

Claire needed more. "So, you met at that conference, had dinner, and three months later she's texting you very explicit messages? Ben, I'm not a fool. You haven't talked to me like that in years. That is not how 'friends' talk to each other. That was—"

Ben cut her off. "Claire, stop. You're making too much of this. It was just texting. It was harmless. We have never done anything. I admit we probably let things get out of hand. But Claire, she's married. She has a family. We never even thought about taking things further. You are my wife, Claire. I have never been unfaithful to you and our vows. You must believe me."

Ben's "innocent" text messages were now etched in Claire's mind. She quoted them as if reading from a script: 'My day has been unbearable without the soothing sound of your voice.' Really, Ben, that's not the way I talk to any of my male friends. You call that innocent?

"And your reply…'if only we had another lifetime.' Who are you? You haven't talked like that since we were dating."

Ben wished he could be transported to that other lifetime. He couldn't think of how to dig himself out of this mess. "Claire, I'm sorry you had to intercept those texts. And I know what it must look like. Can't you just believe me? I got caught up in what seemed like harmless friendship. It really is nothing, and she's definitely not worth coming between us. Will you let me make this right, Claire?"

"It's not that easy. We need counseling. I talked with a marriage therapist today. They can take us, but we both have to be all in."

Ben cringed at Claire's words. He didn't see the need to drag a shrink into their relationship issues.

Claire continued. "This is not just about the messages and your…non-affair. It's about us, our relationship—whatever that even means anymore."

Inwardly, Ben protested. Their marriage was no better or worse than those of his friends at the club. This was a stupid slip on his part. He could undo it and they could move on.

Claire's words rang with urgency. "Ben, I wake up every day fighting off loneliness and depression. We have grown apart and this just proves it. If we want this marriage to work, we need counseling. Please, Ben, won't you do this for us? For our family?"

Ben finally spoke. "I just don't see how a therapist can help. I'll call Bridgette tomorrow and end it, forever. That will be that. You know that if we go into therapy, the news will get out. Do you really want everybody talking about our marriage problems, Claire?"

They fell silent, then Ben started in again, sweetening his tone. "I had no idea that you were waking up depressed every day. Honey, why don't *you* go for therapy? You'll feel better about everything if you can get your depression under control. No wonder this day has been so hard for you."

"Ben, are you completely clueless? This day has been devastating. I learned that my husband is more connected to another woman than to me. That's been my day. I will go to therapy, Ben. And if you want to stay in this marriage, I suggest you go with me. Right now, I'm going to my room. I think you'll be more comfortable on the couch tonight."

Claire angrily heaped pillows and blankets on the couch. "And, by the way, I didn't fix dinner tonight. I was just a little preoccupied. Find some leftovers or starve. I really couldn't care less. Goodnight!"

Ben cringed at the sound of the slamming door.

SCIENCE

# Anatomy of a Marriage

*Few are those who see with their own eyes and feel with
their own hearts.*
—Albert Einstein

As a marriage therapist, I feel deeply with one couple after another, as they unravel their stories of despair, loneliness, betrayal, and lost love. And, though I've heard hundreds of accounts of relationship failure, I'm still shaken and saddened by Ben and Claire's tragic tale. Their story is far too common. The couple that had it all was blindsided by betrayal.

You may be asking yourself, "So what does Ben and Claire's story have to do with me? My relationship is not in crisis. I can't imagine us ever splitting up or betraying each other; I'm in this for life. I just want to make my marriage better."

Ben and Claire were deeply in love throughout the first years of their relationship. They had deep convictions about fidelity and commitment. Like people you may know—and the hundreds of couples in crisis who have come to me for therapy—Ben and Claire are representative of more than half of all married people.

Losing the love we once cherished is a natural disaster. It can happen to any of us unless we take action and learn how to create secure attachment. We can learn from Ben and Claire's mistakes. Through their pain and progress, we can learn how to protect our most valuable asset, our marriage.

If your relationship is now on a firm foundation, it is the perfect time to read this book. By learning how to emotionally communicate and prioritize, you can protect and grow your love relationship. If the foundation of your relationship is already beginning to shake, this book will help you prevent the impending tsunami. The earlier in your relationship that you put this book's principles into practice, the better.

Most of the couples I sit with are in disbelief about their relationship crisis. Many are children of divorce who vowed it would never happen to them. It seems inconceivable that the overwhelming love and affirmation that brought them together could turn into fear and self-protection.

Ben and Claire are attractive, successful, and blessed with beautiful children. They have deep family values and the respect of their friends, colleagues, and community. What went wrong? How could their stable life be so quickly and easily compromised? Ben and Claire were stunned that "this could happen to us."

So what makes love last?

Until recently, scientists have been reluctant to take on that question. The issue seemed too complex and difficult to fit into the confines of their scientific method. Not until recently has the behind-the-scenes science of attachment become part of a growing therapeutic movement. The science of love is now being acknowledged and practiced all over the world. Emotionally Focused Therapy (EFT) has been recognized by the American Psychological Association as a scientifically validated form of couples therapy—a claim that few forms of therapy can make.

A growing body of research outlining the effectiveness of EFT now exists, proving that "couples therapy" works. Studies have found that 70–75 percent of couples move from distress to recovery and approximately 90 percent show significant improvements.

Neuroscientists now know that our brains are wired to connect with others. Humans are created to pair bond, and evolutionary biologists now agree with this fact. We can no longer sidestep the truth that our health and wholeness depend on having at least one unconditional, emotionally connected love relationship.

Emotional connection may be a foreign concept to you, maybe even a scary one. Many have spent a lifetime trying to control their emotions. I'm not suggesting reckless emotional release. I *am* suggesting, though, that the key to connection is in how we express and validate each other's emotions. As this book progresses, you'll watch Ben and Claire as they struggle with (and sometimes "stuff") their emotions. I will walk you through the science driving their responses and reactions.

It is emotion—"energy in motion"—that motivates us to bond with each other, or, when our foundation of love is threatened, to tear each other apart. We seek out the person we love to give us emotional comfort when we are lonely or in distress. Historically, most scientists, philosophers and theologians have tried to take emotion out of the equation of human wholeness. We believe that it's time to give emotion the place it deserves in creating health, love and happiness.

Recently, I had the opportunity to talk to a group of Wall Street leaders about the keys to lasting relationships. I needed a solid topic that would resonate with them and pull at their heartstrings. Suddenly, it came to me: *emotional poverty*. Convinced I had coined the world's next great catchphrase, I was surprised to find a fascinating article in the *Yale News* on "The Price of Emotional Poverty."

The author stated, "In wealthy communities like Yale, we may

14

not struggle with lack of material resources, but we do have some of the same emotional hunger. Our insecurity is manifesting itself in our sex culture, in our disturbing lack of inner peace and in our inability to get beyond superficiality in many of our friendships."[1] He could have been talking about Ben and Claire. Or people you know. Or people you may become.

Emotional poverty is a result of the inability to bond or connect emotionally. It is emotion, not intellect or wealth, that is the most important motivator and security-maker in life. The sad thing is, most of our mindset in education is that we can *think* our way out of problems and into prosperity.

The story and science of this book are organized around one basic concept, and when you understand and practice it, it will protect and grow your love relationship for a lifetime. The concept is so simple that infants know how to do it—yet, it is so absent from our culture that it frustrates and eludes the brilliant physicians, lawyers, entrepreneurs, and business leaders that show up in my office for therapy.

A secure marriage depends on a secure emotional bond with your spouse. That is the secret to lifelong love. And it is within your reach.

Way too many really smart people have their personal lives and careers destroyed because they do not understand the ABC's of making relationships loving and secure. Most of us live with an illusion about what love is and what makes it last. Not seeing it clearly, we settle for an imitation. We can have so much more. It just takes learning and practice. Stay with me on this journey. I will show you how to take your relationship to the next level. You will learn to love more securely and fully, and you will find emotional connection with the one you love.

3

STORY

# Anticipating Therapy

*Have enough courage to trust love one
more time and always one more time.*
—Maya Angelou

Claire couldn't break loose from the knots of the sweat-drenched sheets.

"No, Ben, you can't take the kids. Jake, Leslie, don't go with him."

"Mommy, help me. I don't want to leave you. I don't want a new mommy."

Claire sobbed helplessly as her daughter slipped through her arms. "Stop, Ben. Let go of her!"

Though in a deep sleep on the couch, Ben was awakened by Claire's shrill scream. He glanced at his watch: three a.m. Within moments he was at her bedside, shaking her awake.

"Claire, it's okay. It's just a bad dream. Wake up. It's okay!"

Claire's eyes were wide with fear. "Where are the kids? Where are they, Ben? Where have you taken the kids?"

"Claire, they're fine. They are staying with your sister, remember?" His hand rested gently on his wife's arm as tears filled his eyes. *Oh my god, what have I done?* Shame closed in on him as his mind churned through the events of the previous day. He was trying to figure his way out of the mess he'd created, trying to understand how his friendship with Bridgette had turned his life upside down. *It was a friendship. It was never meant to ruin my relationship with Claire and the kids.*

Ben offered to make tea, and soon the two of them were sitting in the kitchen, sipping in the warmth, hoping for comfort. Uncomfortable silence hovered over the table. Neither could see clearly to the other side of this nightmare.

Gradually, Claire's breathing slowed and color returned to her face. With robotic motions, she put their cups in the sink and shuffled away. Claire was numb. Ben glanced at his watch again. He had to get back to bed. Tomorrow's patients would demand his alertness. He slumped past the couch and followed Claire to their bedroom, hoping that she would let him into their bed without argument. The king-sized bed looked utilitarian rather than invitingly plush.

*One bed, two different worlds.*

Claire awakened after a restless few hours, relieved that Ben had slipped out without waking her. Her nightmare remained fresh in her mind. Its vivid reality sent a ripple of chills throughout her body.

Claire showered and dressed in a fog of sleep deprivation. Cozy sweats and a ponytail was the best she could do today. She glanced at her watch. She knew her sister must be dropping the kids off at school right about now. Claire and Steph had agreed to meet for coffee at nine. How would she muster the energy to share her thoughts and fears and feelings with Stephanie?

She turned in to the Latte Loft on East First Street and pulled down the visor's mirror, not surprised by the unsightly mess staring back at her. She slapped on some lipstick and wiped the black smudges from under her eyes. *Deep breath*, Claire coached herself as she stepped out of the car and into her sister's outstretched arms.

"I love you, Sis."

Claire and Steph sat in silence in a quiet corner of the café until the server came, took their orders, and disappeared.

"I'm so afraid, Steph. I don't get it," Claire began, her composure instantly gone. Tears filled her eyes. She managed to get words past the tight lump in her throat. "I've tried . . . I think . . . I've been a pretty good wife and mother. Why would he fall for someone else? What's wrong with me?"

"I hate him for doing this to you," Steph said vehemently, "but let's not jump to conclusions."

"But Steph, those texts. There was really scary stuff in those words. Kind of like they were . . ." Claire could barely choke out the words ". . . soul mates. Like they were emotionally connected. I had forgotten Ben even had emotions."

Though she mustered a tiny, worn-down snicker to accompany those last couple of words, she did not feel the least bit flippant. *How could Ben be so intimate with another woman and not with me?*

"That's how he talked to me when we first fell in love. Remember? That's why it's so scary. I totally recognize this stuff. It used to be directed at me. He adored me."

"That he did," Steph said. "He couldn't stop bragging about you and your work—your photos and all the awards you earned. It was pretty clear to everyone that he was crazy about you."

"Hopefully, that wasn't all he loved about me, 'cause I sure don't do much of that anymore. I can't remember when I last picked up my camera."

"Don't be ridiculous. It was everything. From the way you looked to the way you so beautifully fit into his world. Don't you remember, Claire? You made pretty much everything better in his life. You were amazing."

"I *was* amazing. And now I guess it's Bridgette. Even her name makes me sick."

"Stop it. You are still amazing, Claire." Stephanie paused, grabbed Claire's hands in hers, and repeated the affirmation. "Claire, listen to me. You are still the same incredible woman Ben fell in love with." She paused, hoping that would soak in. "Ben's just gone a little—well, he's just gotten a bit off track." Stephanie fought through her anger and searched for comforting words. She had to put aside the disgust she felt for Ben at that moment. Right now, Claire needed her to be positive and encouraging.

"This is so confusing, Steph. Why couldn't he just tell me if he needed more from me? Instead he goes off into this private world of his."

"And the messages . . . I just can't get over how he was with her. He seemed . . ." Claire's head dipped toward the table to conceal her embarrassment. "He seemed real, I guess. You know, open and honest. I've begged him for years to let me into his world, and now he's sharing himself with another woman. Why her? Why couldn't he give me a chance?" Claire remembered the countless fights where she had pleaded with him to show some emotion, to let her know how he actually felt about things, to respond to her. He had been quick to share his thoughts, but never his feelings.

"Sounds like Dad, huh? Don't you remember Mother screaming at him? He would just stand there, stone-faced. Then he'd spew all that logic out on her. Remember, Claire?"

"Oh yeah, that used to make Mom crazy mad. She doesn't even react anymore, though. I guess we all learn eventually. Just to deal with our stuff. But Steph? Please don't tell Mom about this mess. I can't deal with her right now."

"Yeah, I get it. You need to worry about yourself right now and

19

Mom would freak. Then she'd get judgmental. Besides, we don't want to reactivate all her stuff. No, Mom definitely doesn't need to hear about this."

They both knew how their mother would react. It would be cruel to have her relive her own pain of betrayal. By the time Mom had learned of their father's two-year affair, it had ended. She'd decided to quietly sweep it under the carpet. She had chosen denial as a means to survive. Any coaching she would have for Claire would be to do the same—ignore until it blows over. Mom took her vows seriously: *for better or for worse.* She'd expect no less from her girls.

Claire escaped for a moment into the soothing aroma of her latte. The soft rumble of voices around her helped to quiet the clutter in her head. She reminisced about the many times she and Ben had sat at that very table when they were dating. *It was so good!*

"I've got to figure this out, Steph. You know, in some ways this seems worse than if he'd just gone after her for sex. Do you think Ben fell for someone else because we stopped making love?"

"What? You still have sex, don't you?" Claire and her sister hadn't talked about their sex lives much. It had seemed a little too personal.

"Well, yeah, we still do it. But it's not like it was. Oh my god, Ben used to be ravenous for my body. Keeping up that pace would have killed me."

Steph didn't see that one coming from Miss Prim-and-Proper. She exploded in a laugh. "Okay, that's a visual . . . "

"It was probably more me. You know how it is once you have kids. You're exhausted. You just want to crash after a sixteen-hour day. The thought of sex just doesn't come up as often."

Claire tried to remember the last time they had made love. Over time, their daily routine had gone from almost nightly to weekly, then lessened from there. Eventually Ben had tired of her frequent rejections and backed off. Monthly sex had become their new normal. Now, in spite of what he'd insisted, Claire couldn't help but wonder if he was getting it from that other woman.

Claire and Stephanie sat in the café for a couple of hours. Steph gave Claire the space she knew she needed to just be. She was there for her sister, listening, supporting, occasionally reaching out to hold Claire's hand.

The beep on Claire's phone reminded her that she would soon need to pick up Jake and Leslie, and she called for the check.

"It's on me," said Stephanie, grabbing a final hug.

"Thanks again, Sis, for keeping the kids last night, and this, and . . . " The lump in her throat caught the rest of her words. "You know. You're a lifesaver."

Claire regrouped as she approached the school parking lot, hoping she could get in and out unnoticed. She pulled it together for the kids, who flew into the car talking a mile a minute. Leslie's enthusiasm was contagious. She kept her first-grade teacher and her fellow students quite entertained. Jake couldn't get a word in if he tried. His reserve made him seem much more like his dad. Quiet, more withdrawn. Claire could tell he never stopped thinking, but she wasn't sure what he was thinking *about*. He was a mini-Ben. *Gosh, why do they make it so difficult for us?*

As Claire pulled into the garage, she nearly hit Jake's haphazardly parked bike.

"Watch it, Mom. You trying to wreck my bike?"

"Well, if you're going to leave your bike there—" Claire stopped herself midsentence, aware that her words and tone were harsher than he deserved. *Pull yourself together, Claire. Jake certainly isn't to blame for Ben's wrongdoing.*

"Okay, kids, let's grab a snack and take a look at your homework. You've got a swim meet at five. Dad's meeting us there. And afterwards, it's your pick for dinner."

Claire snuck over to Leslie, enveloped her petite frame and smothered her with smooches. Jake played hard-to-get but succumbed to mom's persistence. Claire could feel her heartbeat slow, regulate, as she soaked in their goodness.

Later on, as they drove to the pool, Jake entertained himself with a video game. He could taste his near victory over his online opponent, but his sister kept babbling and trying to grab the controls. "Knock it off, Leslie. Play your own game. Mommmmm, tell her to back off!"

"Come on, you guys, can't you get along for ten minutes?" Claire snapped. "Is that too much to ask?"

The kids quieted, taken aback by Claire's uncharacteristic sharpness. Leslie wiped a tear, careful that her brother couldn't see. Just a hint of displeasure in her mom's voice was enough to trigger her sensitive spirit. Jake, on the other hand, was fairly unmoved by Claire's crabbiness.

"I'm sorry for yelling. We're almost there now . . . Let's just settle down and relax."

Easier said than done. Claire's thoughts raced. She worried about Ben's whereabouts. Was he texting with that other woman at this very moment? *Stop it. I can't keep second-guessing him. I'm starting to act like a crazy woman.* Claire expelled a heavy sigh, but it didn't help liberate her from negative thinking. She had always disliked the jealous-wife persona. But how was she supposed to wear this new identity? How did a woman who has been cheated on behave?

Jake's urgency interrupted Claire's ruminating thoughts. This spacey behavior was so foreign to Claire and to the kids. *I have to get control of myself. This is ridiculous.* "Mom, what is with you?"

Jake asked, shaking her out of her reverie. "You've passed, like, five parking places. Just stop. I gotta get out and get warmed up."

"Okay, I'll let you out here, Jake. We'll see you over there."

Claire parked, plastered on her best public smile, and once again assumed her identity as a super-mom. She fumbled with chairs and grabbed Jake's left-behind swim cap and goggles, then grabbed Leslie's hand with her free one and headed across the grassy field toward the pool deck.

Ben had arrived on time—a rare occurrence for him these days. He spotted Claire juggling what seemed enough paraphernalia for the entire swim team and jogged awkwardly over to lighten her load. He set up a chair for Claire a safe distance from his. She smiled cautiously, appreciative of Ben's courteous gesture. The pool's perimeter filled in with familiar as well as new faces. Jake sprinted toward a cluster of teammates across the pool, his classic "Hi Dad, bye Dad" trailing behind him.

Searching for small talk, Ben complimented Claire on her sweater. "It's really a great color on you."

Claire kindly responded with the evening's weather forecast. She knew the conversation was absurdly mundane. *Safe, but oh so boring.* She scrunched down in her chair, feeling certain that the world around her must sense their distance.

She noticed Ben's blank stare. *He is lost again, hiding in his own world. What does he think so intently about when he "goes away"?* Claire watched her handsome husband brush the hair from his forehead and adjust the bridge of his dark glasses. Then she traced his stare. *Is he looking at that blonde across the way?* Claire lost control of her thoughts and feared the worst. *Is it even possible? Is that Bridgette over there?* Her throat tightened, yet she managed to blurt out the words. "Are you staring at that woman, Ben? Is that her? Is that Bridgette?"

23

Ben's day had been hectic and he felt drained. Relaxing at his kids' swim meet could have felt great on a different day. Conversation about the weather didn't hold his attention. He checked out, shut down, walled himself off—from Claire, from those around him, and from himself.

For Ben, it had been a rough couple of days. The humiliation of being thrown out of his own bed hadn't helped. And then there was the shame that he hadn't been able to shake; it had washed over him most intensely when he had awakened Claire's sweat-drenched trembling body from a nightmare. Regardless of the innocence of his relationship with Bridgette, he had clearly triggered a deep fear in his wife.

But this. This was something Ben couldn't tolerate. Claire's words, thankfully unheard by anyone but him, reverberated. *Is that her, Ben? Is that Bridgette?*

"What are you talking about?" Ben replied angrily, his face reddening. He rose and stormed off toward his car. *Will Claire ever let up on me? Can't she see I'm trying? Damn it, can't she give me a chance?*

Ben found his car boxed in by those of other parents. He felt trapped. He paced, kicking the stones in his path and cursing under his breath. He'd understood that his attendance at this meet was imperative, and not just for the kids' sake. The sooner he could smooth things over with Claire, the better. He had hoped that his best behavior would excuse him from couples therapy, but Claire's behavior was absurd. He wouldn't be subjected to her outlandish jealousy, and he certainly wouldn't share the intimate details of his feelings for Bridgette with her, let alone some therapist. He'd just stuff away his feelings for Bridgette and move on. Claire would have to get a grip on her emotions.

Ben could barely think straight, but he did think about his kids. They would both be swimming soon. He wouldn't miss their special moments because of Claire's insecurity. He'd watch them from a different vantage point, that's all. As far as he was concerned, Claire could just stew.

As Claire watched Ben storm off, she panicked. Would Ben actually leave without seeing the kids swim? Did she push him too far? She was scared by her own emotions. How could she love and hate this man in the same moment? How could she hope and despair all in one breath?

The pool blurred before her. Claire knew that Jake was on deck. *Come on, Claire, you can do this. Focus.*

After what seemed an eternity, the meet ended. Ben and Claire met in front of the concessions stand and shared sheepish glances. Once again they looked like a perfect couple as their daughter bounded toward them for hugs, and their son for high-fives.

They had dinner at La Hacienda, the kids' favorite. Ben and Claire avoided eye contact and managed to relax into conversation with the kids. Once they got home and the kids went off to their rooms, however, it was a different story. They had to address what had happened at the swim meet.

"I know, Ben, that it must seem ridiculous for me to even wonder if a random woman across the pool could be her. I just can't get those messages out of my mind. I have no idea what you're thinking or planning." Claire paused and carefully chose her words. "Are you still talking with her?"

"It's over with her, I promise."

Claire felt so vulnerable. "It's hard, Ben. I just don't know how to get through this on my own. I try to push it away, but it's always there." Claire braced herself, anticipating Ben's next words. Her heart shot out a prayer: *Please God, don't let him give up on us. Don't let him leave me!*

Anger drained from Ben. He felt unfamiliar compassion for Claire. "I'm sorry, Claire. I don't get it. I just don't understand why you can't trust me. We can't live like this. I can't be falsely accused every time another woman crosses my field of vision. That's not going to work for either of us." He sighed deeply. "Claire, if you really believe therapy is the way through this, I'll go."

*What have I agreed to?* he thought as he heard himself speak the words, but he continued. "You find someone good, not a quack, and we'll give it a try. Would that make you happy, Claire?"

Claire breathed a hopeful sigh of relief.

part two
# trauma

## Face-to-Face
## with Our Enemies

THERAPY

# Defending with Denial

*How often it is that the angry man rages
denial of what his inner self is telling him.*
—Frank Herbert

I ushered Ben and Claire into my office on Thursday afternoon at three. As is often the case in initial sessions, they were both nervous and apprehensive. And, of course, bound up in tension.

**Therapist:** I want to spend some time talking with you about your relationship and what's happening with you both. Claire, you look really, really upset. What's happening with you right now?

**Claire:** Well, we've been married for ten years, and a week ago I found text messages on Ben's cell. They were from another woman. They were horribly explicit. From the tone of the messages, it seems obvious he's having an affair. He says he's not, but I don't know what the hell else you'd call it.

**Ben:** Wait a second, wait a second. This is . . . I told you, Claire, I have *not* had an affair. I did *not* cross a sexual boundary.

**Claire:** Well, what the hell would you say those messages were?

**Therapist:** Okay, let's just slow this down a little bit. I understand, Claire, that this is devastating for you now. So say more about—

**Claire:** (*Loudly*) We're married, we have two kids, we're active in our community! And then there's your practice. Half the town knows you 'cause you've seen their kids. You bet this is devastating!

**Therapist:** So, it feels like your whole world is falling apart right now and you're melting down on the inside. You just want Ben to understand the magnitude of what he has done.

**Claire:** (*Nodding*) Yes, that's right.

**Therapist:** So, tell me what happened. Tell me what you discovered and how this has so rocked your world.

**Claire:** Well, I'm in bed a week ago, foolishly dreaming, or remembering, I guess . . . how ridiculous . . . remembering our first year together. Actually having really fond memories of us at the beginning of our marriage. My phone is vibrating like crazy all over the nightstand. I realize it's not even my phone. It's *his* phone. I pick it up and glance at it and assume it's a wrong number. The messages I'm seeing are clearly not for *my* husband. And then I see Ben's name in the message. And whoever this is, she knows him. She knows him, and she's talking to him like she's known him for a long time. It was awful.

**Therapist:** So what happened in you when you saw those messages? What did it feel like?

**Claire:** I was confused. I couldn't even make sense of it. I mean, this couldn't be happening to me. Ben was at work. He's a doctor. He was seeing his patients.

**Therapist:** So you were confused. You couldn't believe this was happening to you?

**Claire:** Yeah, I was so confused. How did this happen?

**Therapist:** And in that confusion, what were the emotions you felt?

**Claire:** I was terrified.

**Therapist:** You were terrified.

**Claire:** I was terrified. I was so confused. How did this happen?

**Therapist:** *(Repeating her words back to her)* "How did this happen?" "I can't believe it." "How could this happen to us?"

**Claire:** *(Taking a deep breath)* Yeah, how could this happen to us?

**Therapist:** So, Ben, when you hear Claire talking about being so afraid and so confused that this could happen to you two, what's happening in you as you hear her?

**Ben:** Well, I don't know what to say. It just feels like she's way overreacting. I've tried to reassure her that this text relationship is over and that we did not get sexually involved. I mean, I don't understand what she's so worked up about.

**Claire:** *(Sharply)* You said it was over, and I'm supposed to just believe that it's over? I never even saw this coming. You lied about it and now you say it's over? Maybe you're still lying to me!

**Therapist:** Yeah, so for you Claire, this is so upsetting because you saw the text messages, right? And this has had a devastating effect on you.

**Claire:** They were awful. Ben hasn't talked to me . . . You haven't talked to me that way, Ben, in ten years. How could you talk that way to someone else? To another woman? And say it was nothing? It doesn't make any sense, Ben. How could you do that to me—to our family?

**Ben:** You have to understand, Claire. We worked together. We were in training together. You have to understand that people who work together get close. They talk about their lives and they get close. And yes, we got very, very close.

**Claire:** Close? Is that what you call it? You told her that you love her, that you were thinking about her and missing her!

**Therapist:** So, again, let's slow this down. So when you hear that, that he got close to this other woman—

**Claire:** Her name is Bridgette.

**Therapist:** To Bridgette…I can see how that triggers deep feelings of betrayal in you, right?

**Claire:** Yeah. He promised me. We made vows. He committed his life to me and to the kids, and it didn't include other women. How can I even trust you anymore? How can I even know? I mean, are you even going to work when you say you're going to work?

**Therapist:** So for you, Claire, it kind of feels like your foundations have been rocked. You feel unsafe. You just don't know where you stand anymore.

**Claire:** Exactly.

**Therapist:** So, Ben, when Claire talks about how she is overwhelmed and doesn't know where she stands with you, what happens to you when you hear that?

**Ben:** *(Raising his voice)* That's it! Now I'm pissed. Here we go again. I feel like she's just constantly attacking me and she's suspicious of everything I do. It feels like I can't do anything right. I just don't— I don't know what to do. I'm just getting really angry about her always accusing me of betraying her.

**Claire:** Accusing you of betraying me? Well, what have you done? What would you call this, Ben, if this isn't betrayal? Do you want me to sit back and pretend that I didn't see those messages? They were quite explicit, and frankly, I didn't have the wherewithal or the time to go through your whole freakin' phone and see what else was on there.

**Therapist:** So, for you there's no doubt, right, Claire? The fact that he opened up his intimate life to another woman, whether there was sex involved or not, is a betrayal. This is devastating for you.

**Claire:** I wanted that kind of intimacy from you for a long time, Ben, and you wouldn't let me have it. I just wanted *you*. Until I got tired and finally gave up. Now I only get that from the kids.

**Therapist:** So, what happens to you, Ben, when you hear how badly Claire wanted a deeper connection with you? When you hear how hard and how long she tried to reach you before giving up?

**Ben:** Well…it didn't seem like she was very interested in me. She seemed to be so involved with the kids and with her career . . . It felt like she was always entertaining other women and doing stuff for other people. Frankly, I felt shut down sexually over the years. More and more and more—like she wasn't even interested in me at all anymore. So I don't even know what to say when she says that she wanted a more intimate relationship with me.

**Therapist:** It's baffling, isn't it, to realize that she wanted more intimacy with you and you didn't know how to read her signals?

**Claire:** Wait a minute. When I say *intimate*, I'm not necessarily talking about sex. I wanted you to care about my day and my emotions. I wanted you to be there for me when I needed you. It's been difficult raising our children with so little help from you. You don't ever notice how hard I work for the family.

**Therapist:** Okay, so for you, Claire, you really needed him to be present to your deepest emotions. You needed him to be compassionate with you and to let you know that he understood when you were struggling with all of the pressures of life and motherhood.

**Claire:** Yes, exactly. He had no idea what was going on in my world.

**Therapist:** So the key to deeper intimacy for you was Ben's ability to enter into your emotional world and reassure you. And when you began to believe that he didn't care about how you felt, you stopped sharing your emotions with him.

**Claire:** For sure. It was like I burned out. It's hard to keep going after something . . . It's like hitting your head against a brick wall or just coming up short over and over. And I knew he would never change. I knew he would never really care about my feelings. I mean, you get to the point where your expectations are just . . . Well, it's like there's nothing left. So I stopped.

**Therapist:** You stopped pursuing him after a while. You stopped trying to reach him emotionally.

**Claire:** Yes. I gave up on him. That way, I wouldn't have to feel rejected.

**Therapist:** That way, you wouldn't have to feel rejected. I can just feel how devastating that was for you, to get to that point where you actually stopped doing what you had done for so long, trying to make a connection, trying to reach out to him. In desperation you began to reach out for support in other places.

**Claire:** Yes, I had to. I didn't know what else to do.

**Therapist:** So, Ben, a major shift happened in your relationship at that point, didn't it? When Claire started shutting down and looking for support in other places? It was at that point when you started feeling like Claire didn't care about you, right?

**Ben:** Well, yes. I felt like everyone was more important to Claire than I was.

**Therapist:** So, let me suggest something here. There was a major change in the way you communicated. It's like both of you went silent and felt like the other person wasn't interested in you. When what you each wanted more than anything was to know that the other person loved you. So how did that begin to play out in your relationship?

**Claire:** Well, he was always at work. I will say this: Ben's been an amazing provider. He's taken such good care of our family, financially that is. He spent hours and hours and hours at work, taking care of his patients. He didn't have time for us by the time he got home. He didn't have time for the kids, for me. He was drained. So I backed off a little. I actually felt kind of sorry for him. Maybe it wasn't reasonable to expect anything from someone who has given it all to someone else…to his patients. So I found support in other relationships. I have a sister who is like my best friend. Stephanie and I spend a lot of time together. I mean, I—

**Ben:** Wait just a second. It didn't feel like she felt sorry for me at all. In fact, it felt like she just got more and more critical of me. It felt like I couldn't do anything right. If I was a half hour late from work, she was angry with me. It just felt like, I almost felt kind of incompetent when I was with her. She was constantly on me about not taking care of the kids more. She was constantly on me about not doing more things around the house. I just felt like there was nothing I could do right in her eyes. I could never be as perfect as she wants everything to be.

**Therapist:** So, Claire, you believed that Ben's distance from you had to do with the demands of his medical career. You were actually trying to give Ben space to decompress after work. And Ben, you were feeling that Claire was being critical of you, that there was nothing you could do to please her. Is that right?

**Ben:** Yes. Absolutely. She was just never happy with me. I'd come home dead tired, and she'd immediately give me signals that I was disappointing her again.

**Therapist:** So, when she would be critical of you, what would you do? Would you get angry with her?

**Ben:** No. I'd just go in the study and read a journal or write some notes. Tie up loose ends from my day. The last thing I wanted to do was make it worse by getting angry with her.

**Therapist:** So, Ben, while you knew Claire was upset, you didn't know why. But, instead of risking making her more upset, you contained your feelings of frustration by going into the study and soothing yourself alone?

**Ben:** That's right.

**Therapist:** So, Claire, what would happen to you when you would get upset with Ben about being late or not doing things around the house or with the kids? What would happen to you when he would respond to you by just going into his study?

**Claire:** Yeah, well, that's the story of his life. Run away from it. Run away from conversation. You know, Ben, I'd rather have you get mad at me, to express a little anger if you were ticked off at me. Why not tell me? Or if you were hurt or worried or whatever. Instead, you just stand there and don't respond at all. Whatever I say or whatever I feel, you're just blank, vacant. It's like I'm talking to a mannequin. I'm, like, looking right through you and you're just gone, in some other world. Whether you're physically standing right in front of me or in the study running away from me, you're just *never there!*

**Therapist:** So, Ben's not being there was what got you upset with him in the first place, right? When he would come home late or not be attentive to the kids, it felt like he wasn't there. Then, when you would get upset with him about that and he would walk away from you, it felt like there was nothing left, right? And that's when you would get really angry. And then, Ben, you would shut down even more. Ben, did you ever get angry back?

**Ben:** Well, sure, eventually I couldn't stand it anymore. She just kept nagging and nagging. I would try to take the high road by removing myself. I didn't want to make it worse. But when it went on long enough, I would eventually yell back at her.

**Therapist:** Ben, you tried your best not to react when it felt to you that Claire was being critical and perfectionistic. You would emotionally shut down and withdraw to try and protect Claire from your frustration. But eventually she'd get under your skin and you'd get angry. So that's when things really got ugly, isn't it? When you started accusing each other of not being enough or not doing the right thing.

**Claire:** We could argue for an hour or two. The arguing got more and more intense. It was so frustrating. I just couldn't get him to understand what I was feeling. He would get more and more defensive. Then we would say horrible things to each other.

**Therapist:** Claire, you and Ben were caught in a cycle of arguing. It sounds like you got more and more afraid as you were unable to get him to understand what you were feeling. The more afraid you got, the more you would try to get through to him by expressing your frustration. Eventually, Ben would erupt in anger and that's when you would say things to each other that you'd both regret.

**Claire:** We got really angry and said mean things.

37

**Therapist:** This pattern, Claire, of you pursuing Ben to make a connection and, Ben, you withdrawing so as not to make the argument worse—this is called a *cycle*. When you're in this cycle, you trigger each other, which creates more and more hurt and distance between you until you both wear out and stop arguing altogether.

**Claire:** That's right. (*Ben nods.*) And then we wouldn't talk for hours or sometimes for a day. We have been doing this for years.

**Ben:** I just can't understand why she has to be so critical of me.

**Therapist:** I can hear how painful this is for both of you. When we look at what is happening between you, we see that Claire sounds more and more critical when she is unable to get an emotional response from you, Ben. Is that right, Claire?

**Claire:** (*Her voice now quieter and softer*) Yeah. Well, I wasn't getting his attention. He wasn't paying any attention to me when I was nice.

**Therapist:** So you didn't know what else to do, right? Except try to rivet him, get him to understand how desperately you really needed him. And Ben, you just saw that as her way of invalidating you. It felt like she was saying you were incompetent and not being enough. That must have been so painful for you, coming from the hospital where you were so accomplished and admired. You'd come home and feel like you were constantly blowing it with Claire. That would cause you to withdraw within yourself until you couldn't stand it anymore. And then you guys would get into these awful fights. Is that right?

**Ben:** (*Nodding*) That sounds about right.

**Claire:** (*Voice trembling*) Why couldn't you just tell me, Ben? Why couldn't you just stay there and be with me and tell me that you were tired but you still liked me and wanted to be with me? Why did you always have to go away into the other room? And now, go even further away? Now you've replaced me. You've left me. You replaced me with some other woman, someone you are paying attention to. How can you pay attention to her and not to me? How can you have time for her? That's what I just don't understand.

**Therapist:** That's so difficult, Claire, to understand how you were so desperately trying to reach him for so long and have a connection with him, only to read these messages and imagine these things he is doing with someone else—right? They were the very things you wanted to hear him say to you, right?

**Claire:** *(In a whisper)* Yeah.

**Therapist:** So, when we zoom out and look at the big picture of what has been happening with you, we see an early phase of your relationship where Ben felt buried in the responsibilities of getting a medical career established. And, Claire, you were doing every-thing you could think of to stay emotionally connected with him. You tried to communicate your feelings to him, but he appeared overworked and distant. At some point, Claire, you began to feel like Ben just didn't care about what you were feeling, and you stopped trying to express to him what was going on inside of you. You burned out and shut down. You didn't stop loving Ben, but you did struggle with the feeling that he didn't care about you the way he had before you got married. You felt like you were in second place to his career. And, even though you tried to not overwhelm Ben with these feelings, you grew increasingly resentful toward him and your resentment would come out in ways that made Ben feel like he wasn't measuring up.

**Claire:** That's right.

**Therapist:** And, Ben, you withdrew more and more into yourself. You knew Claire was upset with you, and you didn't know how to make her feel better. You thought that keeping your feelings to yourself was the best solution. In fact, though, that made Claire feel like you were abandoning her for your other interests. When Claire stopped pursuing you, Ben, you felt that she cared about the kids and her friends more than she cared about you. Is that right?

**Ben:** Yeah.

**Therapist:** So, we're going to need to wrap up for today. I just want to help you both understand the recurring pattern I'm seeing. Claire, this pattern starts when Ben feels you are critical of him. Ben withdraws. This causes you, Claire, to feel abandoned and it causes you, Ben, to feel attacked. The reality is that you are both just trying to protect the relationship in different ways. Claire, you are pushing for an emotional connection response from Ben. Ben, you are reacting by withdrawing, which is your way of dealing with Claire's escalated emotion.

I want you to understand that this pattern has been powerful in your lives, probably for a long time. Probably from the beginning of your relationship.

Yes, what Ben did with this other woman has been devastating. We don't want to de-emphasize how important that's been. But it is this recurring pattern, this cycle, that is the greatest enemy of your relationship. We are going to pick up next time with that. I want you to pay attention to that pattern this week and realize that it's that pattern that's going to continue to separate you. It's really important for you two to just hear each other.

Ben and Claire survived their first therapy session with me. As they left the office exhausted, I sensed an unspoken truce between them.

One of the keys to making progress in Emotionally Focused Therapy is helping each person in the relationship understand the cycle they are engaged in. They can only learn to break out of their destructive pattern of arguing when they can both feel and express their deep emotions of fear and hurt and anger toward each other. This takes longer for some couples than for others. In Ben and Claire's case, I was hopeful that enough had surfaced in our first session to help them begin to see themselves and each other differently.

At the same time, I knew that there was much more lurking inside their lives and histories. I hoped that they would glimpse enough possibility in the sessions ahead that they'd be able to trust me and the therapy process. So much depends on that.

5

## SCIENCE

# Trauma, Attachment, and the Cycle

*If you are a card-carrying human being, chances are that you share the same fear as all other humans: the fear of losing love, respect and connection to others. And if you are human, in order to avoid or prevent the pain, trauma and perceived devastation of the loss, you will do anything to avoid your greatest fear from being visited on you.*
—Iyanla Vanzant

In their first session, Ben and Claire revealed three things about themselves that are common to most couples I see. These were the reality of *trauma* in their relationship, the presence of *attachment* issues plaguing their marriage, and a *cycle* of action and response between them.

As is often the case in couples therapy, neither of them was aware of these specific dynamics. Instead, each pointed at the other and named something else as the problem.

The first of these dynamics—trauma—was something Ben would deny and Claire would misidentify.

## Trauma

On December 24th, 2004, in what seemed the heart of paradise, a terrible natural disaster was gathering strength off a sugary sand coast on the Indian Ocean. Sunbathers and locals alike were mesmerized by an eerie occurrence: Within minutes, the tide had receded so far that boats were now sitting directly on the wet sand. Many curious onlookers decided to adventure to the receded water's edge, unwittingly setting themselves up for tragedy.

On its way was a gigantic 100-foot wave known as a tsunami, on course to kill a quarter of a million people. Scientists estimate that this tsunami had the power of 23,000 Hiroshima atomic bombs. Few people were prepared for the devastation of what became one of the largest natural disasters in recorded history.

Life, as people had known it, was changed in an instant. Everything they had clung to for security was wiped out before their eyes. Most of those fortunate enough to survive lost their homes, loved ones, their whole way of life. Entire cities were leveled. Bodies were so numerous they had to be piled into dump trucks and buried in mass graves.

Like thousands of others, Sonali Deraniyagala was celebrating Christmas in paradise, on the island of Sri Lanka.[2] She remembers looking out her hotel window and seeing the first wave move across the beach. She called her husband in from the other room to alert him to the strange happening. By the time he came to the window, the water was flooding the streets at an alarming rate. The couple grabbed their two sons and tried to run ahead of the rising tide. They flagged down a Range Rover to pick them up, but the water level quickly rose above the vehicle's doors and they began to float. Fear overtook them. Like a toy car in a drainpipe, the car turned upside down. Sonali and her husband struggled desperately to hold their boys up in the last remaining air pocket.

Then another current spun them around again, ejecting Sonali from the vehicle.

Before she knew it, Sonali was swept up in the angry ocean that was obliterating everything in its path. She was battered and carried for two miles before she managed to grab on to a tree branch in an attempt to survive.

The horror of her experience was nothing compared to the news she would later receive. Gone forever were her forty-year-old husband, Steve, and her young sons, Vikram and Nikhil. Sonali's parents, who had been staying in the room next door, had lost their lives as well.

Sonali experienced severe trauma. A surreal and gut-wrenching grief consumed her for years as a result of the tragic demise of her most precious relationships. In her book, titled *Wave*, Sonali talks about the years of crazy behavior, antidepressants, and psychiatric treatment she endured before she was able to return to a somewhat normal life.

Trauma is caused by a physical wound or a deeply distressing or life threatening emotional experience. Emotional trauma can be more difficult to overcome than physical trauma. Most of us will never witness our loved ones being swept to their deaths in a tsunami. But many have, or will, experience seemingly less extraordinary emotional events that leave a devastating mark all the same. Emotional trauma should not be taken lightly. It can cause problems that last weeks, years, or even a lifetime. It can be, in psychological terms, an emotional tsunami.

When I met them, Ben and Claire were in the midst of emotional trauma. To each of them, their marriage was escaping their grasp just as a tsunami victim might feel herself slowly losing her hold on a tree branch. They each felt the effects of their emotional tsunami, but neither of them came to me understanding it.

Ben was in denial that trauma had even taken place. He saw his texting with Bridgette as a minor issue, at worst a misstep. He failed to understand that even though it hadn't become physically sexual, it was still an emotional relationship, a connection that he'd formed with a woman who was not his wife.

Claire was right to sense the loss of connection with Ben and to be hurt by the bond he'd formed with another woman. However, she was wrong to identify this other relationship as the tsunami itself. In fact, most infidelities are the result of a deep disconnection that destabilized the relationship years before disaster hit. Claire wanted, somehow, to dial the clock back to a time before Ben's affair; she didn't understand that her marriage with Ben was already destabilized in their first year together.

Or maybe she did. In another way, Claire's mind, body, and heart were telling her—through depression—of the loss she was already experiencing. And Ben felt that loss, too. But he sought, maybe subconsciously, to deal with it by entering into another relationship. Even when a marriage is not ending or heading toward divorce, the experience of gradual distance and incremental disconnection starts to make both parties feel unsafe long before the tsunami can be seen.

The fault line that triggers disconnection early in relationships is formed decades before the couple meets. In fact, relationship security and insecurity begins to be wired into the brain in the first year of life. Our early childhood experiences with relationships influence the way we relate as adults in our marriages.

Early in their relationship, Ben and Claire each experienced the familiar despair of a dying relationship and coped with it in different ways. Most couples have no idea how what they bring to a relationship sets the tsunami in motion. They often feel as if their lives are at risk when the tsunami hits and the relationship may be destroyed. The intensity of their fear can look irrational to people looking from the outside. Couples experiencing the threat of relationship failure feel as if all that they have trusted to keep them safe hangs in the balance. They are overwhelmed with infant-like survival fears.

The answers to what creates the fault lines and fears that cause relationship trauma are found in the science of *attachment*. Ben and Claire, like most couples, did not have a clue that they had attachment insecurities from early in life that contributed to their early marriage disconnection. They also did not understand how a common emotional affair could release powerful feelings that would send them into a spiral of toxic arguments.

## Attachment

Attachment is what bonds us to another human being throughout our lifespan. Attachment feelings and behaviors, not new-love attraction, keep relationships safe and secure. Insecure childhood attachment creates the fault lines that can destroy adult love relationships. These relationship insecurities can shake our foundations when we feel that the person that we are emotionally relying on is no longer safe.

Many young couples in crisis are baffled by how it is possible for their partner to cheat when their relationship started out so "perfect." Mad, passionate, crazy-love attraction can look, smell, and feel like perfection. But the strong emotions we feel in new love relationships can actually mask attachment insecurities.

We build the architecture for our attachment system in our first year of life. During this time, powerful chemicals are released in the brain that cause us to become extremely focused on a parent, or other caregiver, for the love and care we need to survive. We become dependent on our primary attachment figure to keep us safe in the physical world.

How we learn to manage our emotional storms sets the foundation for how successful and self-confident we will become. We need loving reassurance to help us understand our own confusing emotions.

Infants must make sense of what is happening in their internal and external worlds. The helpless child who is totally dependent on a parent has no form of communication other than emotions. It is the child's own verbal and nonverbal emotional cues that provide the signals of what is happening inside of them. For the child to feel secure, a parent needs to respond back, mirroring the child's emotions. This assures the child that he or she is cared for and will be protected when in need.

In the Still Face Experiment (first presented in 1975 by psychologist Edward Tronick and colleagues), a mother is asked to look at her baby without any expression on her face.[3] It is fascinating to watch what the baby will do to get its mother's attention. The baby may giggle, smile, or even point to see if mother will smile back. When mother keeps her gaze of ice, the child's fear alarms go off, triggering a cry for help. When mother still does not respond, a full-blown panic overtakes the child; he or she wails uncontrollably until mother finally, compassionately, picks baby up and provides reassurance. Only then will baby return to a calm, secure state.

Dr. Richard Cohen has proved that infants need the same kind of emotional mirroring from their fathers.[4] They react with the same kind of panic when their fathers stop responding to them emotionally and offer only a still face.

UCLA researcher Allan Schore points out that during the first two years of life, the entire attachment system in the brain is shaped.[5] It is the quality of the emotional communication between parents and child that creates lifelong emotional memories. Where the parent has been responsive, the child is able to create lifetime emotional memories of being loved and cared for. There is a felt sense of belonging and security in this memory. This is extremely important when the child feels insecure with mother or in other relationships in the future. Those who were made to feel secure in their attachment with their parents will be more easily reassured when they are alone or afraid in any situation.

This is the big picture of how attachment is formed and why it has more to do with our health and happiness than anything else throughout our lives. Carrying a deep feeling that we are safe and loved shapes the way we see others and ourselves. It gives us confidence to move through life's difficult challenges. And it allows us to give others the benefit of the doubt when they disappoint us.

When early childhood attachment is insecure, it manifests itself later in life in behaviors we, and our partners in marriage, might not understand.

We have a tendency to repeat our early childhood attachment styles in all of our adult relationships. Those going into an adult relationship with secure attachment foundations tend to forgive their partners more easily than those who are insecure. Those who enter into adult relationships with insecure attachment foundations have trouble forgiving and trusting. However, whether our attachment foundations are secure or insecure going into a new love relationship, we can learn how to build a strong attachment foundation in that relationship.

It is critical that we understand how vulnerable we are to attachment injuries and how to heal them when we are traumatized by a trust violation. You may have picked up this book looking for the solution to that very problem. The answer can be found in *emotional communication*. It is the strength of our emotional communication that heals past attachment injuries and creates strong attachment bonds in adult love relationships.

Injuries caused by a lack of emotional responsiveness can only be healed by emotional responsiveness. No amount of reasoning will convince our wounded emotional hearts that the person who hurt us is safe. We need to feel safe with the person who hurt us, and feeling safe requires a new experience of feeling that person's love and compassion. Many couples find it difficult to repair their relationships when trust has been violated and fear sets in. This is because they want to explain, rather than emotionally express, that they understand and care for each other. Our emotions simply do not respond to intellectual reasons about why we should be feeling better.

*It takes emotion to soothe emotion.*

Without healthy emotional communication, we can easily make our marriage partners feel ashamed of expressing how they need us the most. Without being able to read and respond to our partner's emotional signals, we don't have the capacity to understand how to love and support them. Emotions tell us everything about our deep needs and desires. We instinctively mistrust the expression of a need or a request to be forgiven unless we experience the emotions of the person reaching for us.

Without emotional reaches and responses, we will feel insecure and alone. We'll eventually feel hopeless that we will ever be truly understood. It is difficult to bear the pain of this kind of disconnection. We feel alone when the person we love is not checking in and giving us emotional support. We need to have the ongoing experience of heart-felt understanding.

Feeling emotionally alone in a marriage is the worst kind of pain. We can only bear it so long before our brains learn to shut it off. Even when we are feeling the pain of emotional disconnection, we are more vulnerable than we know to finding ourselves in an affair. Even the most committed heart will light up when a stranger satisfies its starvation for affection.

Whether we realize it or not, we are like X-ray machines,

constantly scanning our partners for emotional signs of their love for us. Most of what we are reading is in our partner's facial expression and voice tone and not in the content of their words. It is the soft voice and inviting face that assure us of their desire for us. In contrast, the most reassuring words delivered with a flat or irritated voice tone will only make us more afraid.

When we do express our emotional need or desire, we expect our partner to be moved and respond. We need to know that if we lead with the first emotional dance step, our partner will follow. If he or she is in the room and not engaging with our emotional reaches, we eventually feel angry, alone, and hopeless.

 Intimacy happens when partners show each other that they are tuned in to their lover's needs and desires. This is a dance we learn over time. Staying connected through the highs and lows of life perfects the dance and increases the feeling of relationship satisfaction.

We have an easier time with the emotional dance in new relationships that have not yet been damaged by disappointment. The more we hurt our partners, the more fearful they become of rejection. They eventually stop giving us emotional signals. We then have a harder time reading them. And we lose confidence in our ability to understand and respond to what they are needing. It is the day-to-day emotional reaching and responding that perfects the glue that bonds couples together.

 Ben never learned the dance of emotional connection. He was taught to soothe himself when he needed a hug. He was overwhelmed by Claire's insecure reaches for him early in their relationship. Eventually she stopped reaching and found comfort with children and friends.

Neither of them knew why this was happening.

This frustration of reaching and not emotionally responding creates the deadly dance that we call the negative cycle.

## The Negative Cycle

Ben and Claire were in a cycle of conflict they could not escape. They needed help to see that the ways they were trying to protect the relationship were only making it worse. If they had come into therapy when their connection first began to disintegrate, they could have headed off the negative cycle that led to the affair. Unfortunately, it took the betrayal to get them to reach out for help. Now, it would take therapeutic skill to help them heal the emotional wounds that had been festering for years.

The negative cycle of communication for Claire was her overwhelming feelings of emptiness, sadness, and anger. She desperately needed Ben to respond to these emotions with compassion and comfort. Like Claire, many of us express our feelings of deep hurt in the form of accusations. This causes the person who has hurt us to protest in self-defense rather than respond to our hurt with compassion. Claire's anger and accusations toward Ben caused him to feel helpless shame, which he expressed with anger and excuses.

Researcher Brené Brown points out that when we are overcome by shame, we are incapable of feeling empathy.[6] Our brains simply cannot simultaneously produce the emotions of shame and empathy.

Although Ben was deeply sorry that his actions had devastated Claire, her attacks turned him inward and inspired feelings of self-loathing that rendered him unable to give her what she needed. As a child, Ben learned how to disconnect from his emotions when he was in relationship trouble. This of course looked to Claire like defensive behavior. Claire was injured even more deeply by Ben's failure to show her empathy and understand the pain that she was expressing. This caused Claire to fire accusations at Ben, which he countered.

Couples in relationship trouble naturally begin grasping for explanations for why they are in pain. It is typical for pursuers like Claire to attack and blame, while withdrawers like Ben quietly hide within themselves. Each partner makes the other the enemy. This attack/withdrawal cycle goes on and on. We call these *negative cycle arguments.*

Ironically it takes two people who love each other to create a negative cycle. The threat of losing the other half of everything and everyone we treasure is devastating! Our brains know that our survival is threatened when our primary love attachment turns against us.

While thoughts take time to develop and express, emotions are instant. When we are in a negative cycle, our emotional responses are lightning fast and cannot be controlled by logic. We must slow the argument down to truly understand and safely express the hurt that is driving the conflict.

It is really sad when we are afraid of or angry with the person we love more than anyone else. The reality is, it is the cycle, not the other person, that is the enemy of the marriage relationship.

There's a lot here to absorb and understand, I know. But at the top level, all you need to remember are these three things: Trauma, Attachment, and Negative Cycle.

Most couples go through a crisis at some point that tests their relationship. It may be a tragedy, an illness, an affair. It may just be a gradual distancing from each other over time. These situations are nothing less than emotional *trauma,* and they can have devastating effects upon each person in the relationship.

This was the situation with Ben and Claire. In response to the trauma she felt from Ben's relationship with Bridgette, Claire responded with overt emotion. In part, this was her way to get from Ben the emotional response/connection she needed. Ben's attachment style, by contrast, was to withdraw in the presence of overt emotion—precisely the opposite of what Claire needed and wanted. They were caught in a devolving cycle.

While I hadn't yet explored their early life experiences, I could see the results of them—this cycle of pursuit and withdrawal, so common in troubled relationships. In our next session, we would begin to explore Ben and Claire's attachment backgrounds.

The form of therapy I practice and advocate is called Emotionally Focused Therapy. The goal of EFT is to help couples slow down and step outside of their negative-cycle arguments and learn to grow secure attachment. When a couple is in a negative cycle, attacks by one or both partners are common. As the therapist, I "catch the bullet" when these attacks happen and reframe or restate the anger from the perspective of the hurt and fear of relationship loss.

While the picture of Ben and Claire's marriage in crisis provides a vivid image of the core issues, the principles of EFT are of great help to couples at all stages of relationship.

You are not alone if you are struggling to find answers for the relationship problems you face. Until recently, there was no scientifically proven therapy to help couples escape the negative cycle by helping them express their deep needs for emotional connection.

Most mainstream methods of working with distressed relationships focus on trying to tone down the emotional storm by problem-solving or changing behaviors. In other words, many traditional cognitive or behavioral therapists try to rescue couples in crisis by trying to get them to think or behave differently. They work on getting their patients to look more logically at what they are fighting about and try to help them find win-win solutions.

They might encourage date nights or more frequent sex. They might try to teach them better communication skills.

But without first healing the emotional injuries driving the conflict, these strategies produce only temporary relief; ultimately, they may even make the disconnection worse. By failing to treat the intense emotional pain of the attachment injury, these therapists are putting a Band-Aid on a deep, infected emotional wound. These unsuccessful fixes do nothing to stem the ongoing disconnection and relationship breakdown, which continue to spiral downward.

The approach of EFT is to help couples understand and manage the emotions they are experiencing, the attachment roots they come from, and the ways they can move forward toward real connection and a fulfilling relationship.

This is what I would endeavor to do for Ben and Claire.

# part three
# **early childhood**

## How Parents Shape Childhood Attachment

6

STORY

# The Birth
# of Connection

*Loneliness and the feeling of being unwanted
is the most terrible poverty.*
—Mother Teresa

*survived the demons of the night,* Claire thought as she massaged her red-rimmed eyes and braced for a new day. She had endured thirteen agonizing days and nearly as many sleepless nights since learning of Ben's affair. She was exhausted. Her emotions had ping-ponged wildly in the week since their first therapy session. Anger and anxiety propelled Claire forward, while fear and loneliness paralyzed her. Sometimes, she wished they could go back, undo what had been done, return to the ordinary life they'd had before. Yet, she knew now the life they used to have was a sham.

The only way through this was forward. Repairing the damage and building new marital foundations after so many years of disconnection would not be easy. And she was already very spent emotionally.

But Claire was determined to win the fight for her marriage.

She shuffled to the kitchen in pursuit of a caffeine fix. The steamy brew would not quench her need to feel loved by Ben, but it would help her cut through the fog and get through her morning. Claire grabbed for the espresso beans. She brushed her bangs from view as her eyes locked onto the pewter-framed wedding photo sitting on a nearby table. Shining eyes and full-faced smiles filled the frame. She remembered how full of love and hope they had both been on their wedding day. Those feelings had been crushed with the discovery of Ben's affair. Claire dropped the frame to its face, wishing away the memory.

Claire made her way upstairs to her sleeping kids. She began with Jake. It was always a fight to start his engine. Leslie was half-dressed by the time Claire made it to her room. Leslie was so much like Claire had been: always a step ahead of her mother's orders, never had to be told anything twice. As a child, Claire had behaved in a manner that she had hoped would be rewarded with praise and love. Jake, on the other hand . . . "Come on, Jake, let's get moving. You're going to be late."

An hour later, with the kids safely at school, Claire tried to find respite in her work. She had to view hundreds of photos for the travel article she was working on, and her deadline was fast approaching. It was imperative that this be her best work. Now, more than ever, the work she loved would have to be more than a hobby—or a source of extra income. If Ben couldn't get it together, she might have to be more financially independent than she'd ever imagined.

Going through the Windy City photos, a family vacation plus business photo-op for her, seemed like it would be a healthy emotional distraction. But the digital images that rose up before her seemed cracked like broken glass. In addition to the Chicago cityscapes, which occupied most of the CD, there were random kid pics. Tears wet Claire's cheeks as she flipped through the images of her family on her screen. The spontaneity of the day in the city had seemed magical. Ben had actually joined her and the kids for a picnic in the park along Lake Michigan. *It seemed like he was happy. Busy, but happy.*

Claire had been determined to create great memories for her kids. She wanted them to know that they were loved unconditionally. More than knowing, she wanted them to feel it. She wanted them to feel safe and adored whether they were in her lap, at school, or falling asleep at night. She didn't want them to ever question hers and Ben's love for them.

She didn't want them to feel unloved, as she had growing up.

Why hadn't her mother found the time to hold her more, to be cheek-to-cheek with her on her lap? Claire vividly remembered the insatiable need she'd had to be with her mother. She had followed closely on her mother's heels, pleading for attention. The more she was ignored, the louder her demands got. And the harder she tried *to be good enough.*

Claire did remember some times when her mother seemed close to her—especially on morning strolls through the park together, an activity they both seemed to delight in. A socialite friend of her mother's had been present on those walks, too, and the women would visit and gossip—but still, Claire had cherished those walks in the park, partly because she sensed that her mother was calm and at peace in those moments.

Several years before the cataclysm with Ben, when the children were still babies, Claire had stumbled upon her mother's journal. Reading it was troubling, but she was glad for the clarity it brought to what she had felt vaguely for years. Her mother's words floated through her mind as if there was no gravity to hold them in place. *How can a baby be so demanding?* her mother had written. *She frustrates me. She's so time consuming.* The simple act of soothing her baby had never come naturally to Claire's mother. The harder she tried, the more frustrated she became. As she described it, it seemed as if baby Claire's rigid little body had mimicked that of her nervous mother.

Claire felt the words in that journal deeply. She felt unwanted. Inadequate. *Perhaps if I had been a better child . . .*

She had never let on that she had seen her mom's journal, but she knew that her own experience of motherhood would be very different. Claire's mother had been annoyed by pregnancy, while Claire had loved being pregnant. The changes in her figure had been a more-than-equitable trade-off for the lives she would bring into the world. With Ben inaccessible during his early career-building years, she had craved the closeness of another. Her babies had filled that need.

Claire's day was wasting away, but she needed some of her precious time to process what she was going through. She turned from her work project and pulled out a photo album from her own childhood. She saw these photos through a new lens. Claire's mother seemed so absent in her presence. *She made holding me look like a chore.* The tight smiles, near grimaces, on her mother's face suggested the disruption Claire had been in her life.

*Certainly I'm reading into these photos. She was a really good mother—wasn't she?*

Claire came to a picture of her dad. Her father, when he was in town, had been the attentive parent. He had tucked her into bed, listened to her prayers, and left her with a kiss on the forehead. His dramatic ritual of ridding the closets and dark corners of monsters would leave Claire and her sister Steph in stitches long after he had closed their door behind him. Their mother would later pass through the hallway and call out a somewhat stern, "That's enough, girls. It's quiet-time now."

Claire came to a realization: *Dad showered me with affection while Mother seemed to disappear at its opportunity.* For so many years, Claire had tried to win her mother's affection by being a more perfect daughter. As an adult, she was bound and determined not to let her own kids down that way. For them, and for Ben, Claire worked hard to provide an ideal life filled with ideal love.

While contemplating all of this, Claire's cell phone rang and startled her. She tensed, remembering the text messages from Bridgette. Reaching for a tissue, she wiped her tired eyes and picked up her phone. The caller I.D. made her stomach sink.

"Hello, Mother."

Claire didn't really believe in premonitions, but she wondered how it happened sometimes that the person you were thinking about suddenly materialized. Or maybe her mother had special powers.

"Of course I remembered you were coming to the kids' school concert tonight," Claire lied. "Sure, that's great. Dad's coming too, I hope." Claire could tolerate her mother when her dad was around to soften her critical edges. "No? Oh, I'm so disappointed. Can't he miss his night with the guys just this once? It's been forever since I've seen him."

Claire wished she could confide in her mother, but that just wasn't the way things were. Once they'd confirmed plans for the evening, she hung up, feeling the emptiness in their relationship.

Ben was livid when Claire reminded him that they'd be spending the evening with her mother.

"This is not a good time. I can't believe you didn't tell her *no*, Claire. You could have said the performance was canceled or something, couldn't you? Do you really want to put up with her third-degree tonight?"

Ben wasn't surprised by Claire's comeback, but the angry edge in her voice was something he wasn't used to.

"Just because you seem to be comfortable lying, Ben, doesn't mean I'll go there. It's not my fault our marriage is a mess. I'm not going to cover your butt with a lie. Maybe I should just go ahead and tell her you've had an affair before she finds out from someone else."

Ben didn't know what to say.

"So…should I tell her we're in therapy to save our marriage?" Claire continued. "What about the D word? Should I throw that in there, too?"

"Calm down," Ben said, finding his voice. "You're being ridiculous now. I haven't said a thing about divorce, Claire. Maybe it's you who wants that, but I said I'd go to therapy. I'm not going for the fun of it. I'm thinking it will actually fix our marriage."

"Then you tell her, Ben. If you want to lie, you tell her she can't come see her grandkids perform tonight because our marriage is a mess. You're just terrified she'll see it all over our faces."

"Fine, Claire, whatever. We'll do it. Trust me, though. She'll find a way to ruin it for you, me, and the kids."

Ben didn't dislike Claire's mother. In fact, he had been somewhat amused by her mastery of the art of illusion. It was eerie, and usually harmless, how she could manipulate a situation, her behavior changing to match her audience. Truth be told, there was something about her that he felt comfortable with. She was matter-of-fact, never getting sidetracked by emotionalism. He was used to that, as his own parents had been cut from the same cloth. With Claire's mother things were clear. You always knew where you stood with her. Like his own mother and father, she was very practical, and Ben liked that.

Even so, he was aware of the darker side of Claire's mother, and couldn't tolerate the negativity she brought into his home. Regardless of his own problems with Claire, he couldn't stand by and see his wife berated. Ben had learned to ignore most of the jabs

Claire's mom directed toward him, but was incensed at the way she treated her own daughter and the effect of this on Claire, who would bite her tongue while fighting back her tears. For as long as Ben had known her, Claire had longed for a better relationship with her mother. He saw the signs, though. Claire's mother never really seemed to like Claire.

That much was obvious. And now he didn't understand why Claire kept trying to please her.

Ben dreaded the evening ahead. He was certain it would not be a positive experience for anyone. *Is this really all my fault? If Claire paid a little more attention to me, maybe I would never have fallen so hard for Bridgette. Bridgette...it's so much easier talking with Bridgette. She always gets me.*

His cell phone chirped, and Ben wondered if it was a text from Bridgette. But his hopes deflated when he saw it was from Claire.

Again? "What the . . ."

Ben's words faded as he read Claire's text reminding him of that afternoon's therapy appointment. *Can this day get any worse?*

Then came another message: "Sorry I was difficult about Mom. Love you!"

*For the life of me, I can't understand the woman's thinking.* Ben let out an exasperated sigh, and proceeded to call Bridgette.

Claire anxiously checked her cell to see if Ben had responded to her apology text. A familiar alarm arose within her as she stared at the blank screen. *That son of a . . .*

Ben's avoidance always brought out the worst in Claire. Pangs of jealousy coursed through her, yet another ugly byproduct of Ben's unfaithfulness.

Should she stop by the office to check on him? Once again, anger and anxiety propelled her forward. But something else gave her pause. *No, I have to trust him,* she thought. *A random visit would surely send him through the roof.*

Ben was annoyed by Claire's persistence. Her neediness. To him, her wildly swinging emotions were an impossible maze to navigate. He didn't grow up around that sort of behavior. His parents, though loving in their way, had been focused on becoming all they could become, achieving their best. They had motivated Ben to do the same. When Ben had showed aptitude for the sciences, they'd paved the way for him to become a doctor, in many people's minds the highest achievement possible.

Growing up, Ben had never gotten sidetracked by emotional stuff. Emotions were unbecoming, unproductive. And now, faced with Claire's emotional pursuit of him, Ben was frustrated and confused.

Silencing his phone for the next few hours would only intensify her neediness. It seemed he could never win with her, so he often said nothing. The truth was, his attention to his patients often left him without emotional energy for Claire. Of course, he couldn't tell her that—it would only trigger her anger and make his life even more unbearable.

Ben knew that a simple reciprocal "I love you" would soothe Claire and avert a deluge of additional text messages. This left him feeling the familiar tug between honesty and appeasement— but he had to say something. Ben winced as he typed the empty words, hoping that they would pacify her.

Peace washed over Claire as she read Ben's reply. Three simple words brought tranquility to the despair of her morning.

Soon Claire was on to her next agenda item—an update for Steph. As she hit #1 to speed-dial her sister, she recalled the ridiculous fight she and Ben had had over the fact that Steph was #1 while he was somewhere around #5 or so. *Oh, brother.*

"Hey, sis, just checking in . . ."

"What's new?" Steph asked.

"Well, I've been working on this family history form Dr. Regier has us filling out. These questions about our childhood seem so irrelevant. And I can't even imagine what breastfeeding has to do with Ben's affair. Steph, I'm not talking about me breastfeeding my kids; the doc wants to know whether I was breastfed by Mother. Hopefully the guy's not a quack."

Claire paused as she was filled with warm and comforting memories of breastfeeding her children. She and Ben had learned in their Lamaze classes that breastfeeding might not be easy for every one. "If it isn't perfect at first, try again," the instructor had advised over and over. "Baby will love and thrive, and so will Mommy." But when the time came, it was perfect. Nursing her kids had been one of the best decisions and experiences of her life.

Steph waited for her sister to continue, somehow understanding that she was savoring the sweetness of her thoughts. The two went on to laugh and cry, feeling the sacredness of each emotion. Claire longed for a secure connection like this with her husband. The easy conversation with Steph amplified the emotional chasm between her and Ben.

Before the sisters ended their call, Steph delivered a few perfectly timed sentences. "It will be okay, Claire. You're tough, remember? You *will* get through this."

Claire wondered, though, if she really would.

Ben finished up with his fourth patient of the morning, a high-spirited severely disabled six-year-old boy. As he paused in the painful memory of his brother Max's all-consuming childhood disease, his chest tightened with deep sadness. Max's story had had a happy ending; the young boy who had just left Ben's examination room would probably not be so lucky. Despite Ben's love for the clarity of medicine—diagnoses based on the factuality of tests and prognoses based on proven data—sometimes he had to face the emotion that the facts triggered in his patients. And in a time such as this, because of Max, Ben felt even more deeply for this boy and his parents. Oh, the pain they would be enduring.

Ben thought about the upcoming therapy session and realized it might force him to revisit these uncomfortable feelings. He picked up his phone and noticed Claire's fourth text message of the morning. She was proficient at pushing his buttons. The therapist had referred to this as typical "pursuer" behavior—Claire's reach for love. Typical perhaps, but Ben saw it simply as annoying. Regardless, he did not want to deal with the consequences of being late to that afternoon's session.

He quickly checked his watch. Still a couple of hours before the appointment. Though Claire's sense of urgency rubbed him the wrong way, he quickly responded with a brief and somewhat curt, "I will be there." He had patients to see and didn't have time for her hovering.

The upcoming appointment weighed on Ben. Last week's session had been rough for him, though he had kept that mostly to himself. Claire's assessment of him as being "unaffected" was far from the truth. He had been hopeful that his early morning solitary runs would be a good release and escape. Instead, they had served only to further test his limitations. His muscles had burned beyond tolerance along with everything else in his being. While he could not begin to sort out or give a name to what he was feeling inside, Ben ran harder, faster, and further to try to distance himself from it, to replace the pain with another kind that he could identify. This pain felt safe to Ben. He would need to find a new level of endurance in order to balance his busy medical practice with the marital therapy process.

Ben imagined what his father had juggled when he and his mother had gone through their marital crisis years back. He kicked himself for having gotten into this mess in the first place.

Ben shook the tension from his shoulders and prepared for his next patient.

Ben and Claire had spent their days so differently. Would they be able to find each other's hearts in the afternoon's therapy session?

7

THERAPY

# Taking the Heat

*People are always fascinated by infidelity because,*
*in the end—whether we've had direct experience or not—*
*there's part of you that knows there's absolutely*
*no more piercing betrayal. People are undone by it.*
—Junot Diaz

Ten minutes before the session with Ben and Claire was to begin, the small brass bell on my door alerted me that someone had entered my waiting room. When I looked at my monitor I saw Claire alone, looking nervous, pouring a glass of water.

I opened my progress notes from the last session and reflected on what is happening in their relationship. I was once again reminded of how an emotional connection outside of marriage can completely destabilize what externally looks like an unshakable fortress.

How is it possible that Ben, once Claire's knight in shining armor, could instantly transform into a villain she can no longer trust? Does his emotional indiscretion really warrant this terrible judgment?

There's a certain insanity in the change in perception of a lover betrayed. The most intimate relationship on earth becomes, in the heat of one moment, the most hateful relationship on earth.

That's not to say that a change in perspective is unjustified—but a marital affair often prompts an intense emotional reaction that transcends reality.

We experience overwhelming emotion when our bond (attachment) with the person we marry is threatened. The level of emotion we experience is affected by how we have been injured by past relationships.

It would be my first goal to help Ben validate Claire's intense emotions of betrayal—even though, from Ben's perspective, he does not think that what he did warrants the judgment and fear that Claire is expressing. The reality is that the emotion is real for Claire: She needs to know that Ben understands and can feel with her the depth of the pain that she is in.

What is vital here is for Claire to experience the kind of emotional validation that her parents were never able to provide. It is just as important for Ben to learn to express his emotions to Claire. If Ben can express, through his emotions, that he understands her injury, she will have a corrective emotional experience with potential to replace her emotional memory of abandonment with a new experience of being emotionally supported.

I heard the bell on my door ring again and saw Ben, arriving two minutes before the session was scheduled to start.

I walked to the waiting room. Ben sat on the chair across from Claire, rather than beside her on the love seat. I greeted them, walked them to my office, and began the work of healing a marriage.

**Therapist:** So let's start here: What have each of you been feeling about your relationship this week?

**Claire:** *(Agitated)* I have been so frustrated. I have been unable to sleep at night. It feels like the ground underneath my feet is shaking. I can't seem to get hold of myself. My trust in him has been destroyed. When I try to text him, he doesn't even respond! And he gets angry whenever I ask him what he's been doing when he's gone.

**Therapist:** It sounds like you are angry and fearful that your relationship with Ben is no longer safe. You can't seem to find a way to get his reassurance, to keep him from pulling away.

**Claire:** That's right. I am the one who has been devastated by what he did, and now he is more distant than ever.

**Therapist:** Okay. Now, Ben, what is happening to you as you hear Claire expressing how fearful she is that she is losing you?

**Ben:** *(With a sigh)* I do everything I can to reassure her that I am not going anywhere. But the more I try to tell her that my relationship with Bridgette is over, the more questions she asks me and the more angry she gets. I have a job to do. I can't always respond when she contacts me. When I *do* try to text her back, what I say never calms her down. All I can do is wait out each wave of anger.

**Therapist:** So you are at your wit's end in trying to understand how to help Claire feel more secure. You seem to get so overwhelmed by her emotions that you shut down and stop responding. Is that right?

**Ben:** I don't know what else to do. When I engage her, I just make things worse.

**Claire:** Engage me!? Get angry *at* me is what you do. *You* should be the one apologizing. *I* am the one who is hurt, but you're acting like the victim. I can't believe that you did this to me and our family!

**Therapist:** Okay, let's slow this down. I can hear, Claire, that his not responding to your emotions cuts you to the core. This wound sounds so familiar. It reminds me of what you told me happens to you when you try to reach out to your mother.

**Claire:** To this day, she ignores how I feel. I have to go to my father to get any understanding. I never thought Ben could treat me the way *she* does.

**Therapist:** Is it fair to say that what's happening between you and Ben now seems like a nightmare that you are reliving? You counted on him to be your safe haven, and now it feels that he is abandoning you when you need him the most.

**Claire:** Yes. It's betrayal and abandonment! What could be worse than that!

**Ben:** What she doesn't understand is that nothing has changed. I am not going anywhere. I made a mistake and have apologized. The relationship with Bridgette is over. She just keeps battering me over and over.

**Therapist:** So, Ben, you feel like you have done everything you can to make the relationship right. You have apologized and have broken the relationship off with Bridgette. You are having a hard time understanding the intensity of Claire's fear and mistrust.

**Ben:** It doesn't match the crime.

**Therapist:** So you are trying to make sense out of her reaction in light of what you did?

**Ben:** What else is there to understand?

**Therapist:** That is such an important question. The intensity of Claire's emotion is telling us that there is a deep injury in her that needs healing.

**Ben:** I don't know what I'm supposed to do about that.

71

**Therapist:** I'm not surprised, Ben, because in your childhood world, emotions were largely ignored. Your father taught the people in your family to pull themselves up by their bootstraps when they were emotionally hurt. Even your mother pretty much went along with this kind of thinking. Does that sound somewhat accurate?

**Ben:** Yeah. It's what I grew up in, though I'm not sure that's entirely true of me today.

**Therapist:** Well, let me go a step further. When you hear Claire expressing her deep, childlike emotional fear, do you find yourself speaking in your father's voice?

**Ben:** *(Slowly nodding)* That kind of rings true. I have my issues with my dad, but sometimes I do hear him in myself.

**Therapist:** So…Ben, what you might not be aware of is that your father's voice is coming through you when you react to Claire. Your disapproval of her emotion makes her feel shame for having emotion in the first place. And, when Claire feels ashamed of feeling hurt, she gets angry and vindictive. She wants you to feel what she is feeling because of what you did to bring up this wound in her. Inside, you may feel hurt when she lashes out at you—but on the outside, you look unshaken. She has no way of knowing that her hurt is having any effect on you. Does that make sense?

**Ben:** *(Nods)*

**Therapist:** In your family, the safe thing to do was to own your mistake and move on without expressing any emotion at all, right?

**Ben:** Yes, I guess so. It was never accepted in our house to express our emotions that way. We would say we messed up and then just move on.

**Therapist:** With Claire, this strategy is badly backfiring on you. When you look unaffected by her emotional pain, she panics and comes back even harder with anger and accusations. And that's when the cold scientist in you comes out. You give her a look of disapproval and go cold and silent. You erect a wall that is impossible for her to breach.

So, what is happening with each of you as I describe this big picture of how you injure each other in your arguments? What are you thinking?

**Claire:** You're right. He does become a sort of cold, mad scientist. I don't understand how he could not be more compassionate about the pain that I am in. It is everything that I grew up with—the nightmare that I never wanted to relive.

**Therapist:** But it makes sense, doesn't it, how terrifying it is for Ben to feel like there is nothing he can do to help you with your emotional pain, other than try to be logical?

**Claire:** Logic is the last thing that I need right now. I need to know that my husband has a heart. That he deeply cares about the hurt that he has caused me. It just sounds like he is trying to let himself off the hook and leave me alone to suffer.

**Therapist:** Of course it does. His emotionless apologies give you no way of knowing what he really feels about you or about how sorry he is.

**Ben:** *(Angrily)* That is just not fair! I did break down right after she found out. I could not control my tears. I repented for what I had done. What more does she want?

**Therapist:** I can just imagine what it was like for you, Ben, to feel like you were at a breaking point. You were so overwhelmed by your own regret that you uncharacteristically erupted with an emotional apology. But now it feels like you two should return to the logical, normal dialogue you are both used to. Am I right that

that moment of emotion was uncomfortable for you? How did you feel?

**Ben:** I think I just was under a great deal of stress—

**Therapist:** No, Ben, I'm asking what you *felt*, not what you *thought*.

**Ben:** Okay, well…The truth is, I felt kind of embarrassed for the tears. I felt out of control. I wanted to climb out of that emotion and get back to normal.

**Therapist:** *Normal?* What is normal?

**Ben:** Kind of like what you were saying. Back to a level of control.

**Therapist:** Rational control?

**Ben:** Yes.

**Therapist:** *(Pausing to let the understanding sink in)* What is important for you both to understand is that this betrayal has opened up wounds *in both of you* that date back to your early experiences with your parents. Emotional reassurance has never been a foundation in your marriage.

Now, I need to tell you both something that might be hard to hear. Now that Claire has been traumatized by the affair, *it is impossible for the two of you to go back to life as you knew it.* Claire cannot address her emotions without your help, Ben. She has been shaken too deeply. Her lifelong fears about being left alone in her emotional pain, when she needs to be loved the most, have been activated.

Trauma expresses itself in a number of ways. Claire may become hyper-vigilant, looking over her shoulder at everything you do and say. She may mistrust you, question you, and demand emotional transparency. And Ben, this is important. Her fears must be answered with emotional, not logical, reassurance.

I understand, Ben, that this is not something you feel comfortable with or are even capable of doing on a consistent basis. It is vital, however, that you understand—both of you—that *emotional communication is the foundation for healing this injury and for establishing secure intimate attachment between you.*

Here's the good news. As I help each of you talk about what you are feeling and you unpack your hurt, you will begin to learn to express your deepest fears without defensiveness and blame. I've seen this happen for other couples. It can happen for you, too. As you hear each other's deepest heart cries, you will heal the hurt of the present and kill the demons of the past. You will learn the emotional language of love that can help you fill the loneliness and establish your relationship in a lifetime of loving safety.

We were close to wrapping up. I sensed that Claire still wanted to lower the boom on Ben for the affair. And I knew that Ben was mostly bewildered, because he was simply trying to live his rational, non-feeling life, as he was taught to do growing up.

And yet I left our time together with an impression that both Claire and Ben were glimpsing something new about each other—something about how the children inside both of them grew up and became the adults they are today.

8

## SCIENCE

# The Science
# of First Bonds

*The bond between a parent and child is the primary bond,
the foundation for the rest of the child's life. The presence
or absence of this bond determines much about the child's
resiliency and what kind of adult they will grow up to be.*
—Jane Fonda

The science of relationships provides great insight into how our adult relationships sometimes go right, but often go wrong.

The bottom line is this: The caregivers that we rely on in early childhood influence our relationships for the rest of our lives.

According to neuropsychologist Allan Schore, the brain grows the foundation of its relational architecture during the first two years of life.[7] The way that a child will relate to others for the duration is built on this foundation.

Infants are unable to survive without the loving emotional attention of an adult, and emotions form the language of infant communication. They are what let caretakers know what the infant needs and feels. Secure mothers are wired to be extremely attentive to the emotional signals of their children. They are attuned to the cries that announce fear, hunger, and pain. They know when their infants want to play. They respond with verbal and facial expressions that mirror their child's emotions. They answer the cries for milk, a hug, or loving comfort.

When our caretakers lovingly respond to our emotional communications, we trust them. We know that they will be there when we need them the most. We learn that it is okay to cry when we are hungry, alone, or afraid. We learn that our laughs and smiles will be greeted by laughs and smiles from those caring for us. This forms a healthy foundation for relationships later in life.

When our caretakers do not respond to our emotional communications, we become insecure. We feel uncared for and unloved. In a desperate attempt to ensure that our survival needs will be met, we cry even louder—or we stop crying altogether. Both behaviors make it difficult to get the love and care we need.

These early "attachment bonds"—interactions with our caregivers—are the glue that holds relationships together. They give us the reassurance that others will not abandon us when we are in need and afraid. They create the feeling of safety inside us that allows us to express our deepest fears, hurts, and inner longings.

Our first parental bonds color our world, painting the way we think and feel about love. Attachment bonds form an internal model of how we expect those we love and depend on to treat us.

Understanding our own love stories, stretching back to childhood, helps us to understand why we keep getting stuck in our adult love relationships.

## Child Attachment Science

Scientists refer to the relationships that we bond with as *primary attachments*. Infants have a primary attachment to their parents, or sometimes other caregivers such as a nanny, a stepparent, or a grandparent. We never lose our need for primary attachment bonds. When we become adults, *we transfer this parental dependency onto a husband or a wife.* If we are single, we may rely on close relatives or friends.

These days, a whole new field of attachment neuroscience is demonstrating how childhood attachment bonds are transferred to adult love relationships. It is not uncommon for people in old age to still be struggling with unmet love needs from childhood.

Like most of us, Ben and Claire grew up with parents who did not understand the new science of attachment. They did not know how important it is to respond to the emotions of their children. They grew up with parents who did not validate their emotions. They were taught to suppress emotions and will themselves to behave better.

Until recently, mainstream psychology offered little understanding of how the bonds formed in childhood shape our capacity to love in adult life. Emotionally controlled adult behavior was the standard for children. Crying and behaving in ways that seemed overly needy, angry, or afraid was seen as disruptive. Parents were expected to train these behaviors *out* of their children.

It's fascinating to read some of the seminal literature on this. As early as 1928, psychologist John B. Watson wrote, in his book *Psychological Care of Infant and Child:*

> Treat them as though they were young adults. Dress them; bathe them with care and circumspection. Let your behavior always be objective and kindly firm. Never hug and kiss them, never let them sit on your lap. If you must, kiss them once on the forehead when they say goodnight. Shake hands with them in the morning. Give them a pat on the head if they have made an extraordinary good job of a difficult task.[8]

As extreme as this kind of childrearing sounds, the idea that children should be taught to behave like emotionless adults persisted through the 1960s. Benjamin Spock taught mothers that picking up their babies when they were crying would reinforce their bad behavior. The famous behavioral psychologist B. F. Skinner viewed infants as blank slates, meriting attention only when they displayed good, mostly non-emotional behavior. The bonding benefits of breastfeeding were largely ignored. In 1971 only 24 percent of newborn infants in the United States were breastfed. As medical research began to reveal that breastfeeding was beneficial to both physical health and emotional bonding, this number gradually increased to 80 percent by 2003.

Rene Spitz's studies and observations in the 1940s established that young children deprived of nurturing human touch and human interaction, though provided with good food, safe housing, proper hygiene, and adequate medical care, would wither and die. He found that babies raised in a foundling home environment under the care of nurses working eight hour shifts, failed to grow and develop. More than a third died. The majority were physically, mentally and socially retarded. Many of them were still living in institutions after 40 years. They were unable to care for themselves because of their early deprivation.[9]

Parental love was clearly the key to infant survival.

John Bowlby, the father of attachment theory, was the son of an aristocratic British family and was raised by nannies. When Bowlby was of an age when he could be expected to behave "properly," he was allowed to interact with his mother at teatime, usually for one-hour periods. Bowlby recalled that when his parents replaced his nanny, he was so emotionally devastated that it felt as if a parent had died. These people simply had no understanding of the importance of bonding for healthy psychological development, or how the loss of a primary bond—in this case, a nanny—could cause immense psychological trauma.

Rejecting the psychological theory of his time, Bowlby began to research the relationship between lack of bonding (attachment) and criminal behavior in children and adults. In 1944, he compared forty-four juvenile thieves with a group of emotionally disturbed non-thieves. Seventeen of the thieves had been separated from their mothers for more than six months before the age of five. None of the emotionally disturbed non-criminal control group had been separated from mom.

Bowlby's research led him to formulate the first theory of attachment, which suggested that all human beings have a need for emotional connection, from cradle to grave, with at least one significant person. He maintained that secure attachment is the foundation on which the emotional life is built and is the basis for lifelong happiness and health.[10]

At first, Bowlby's research was rejected. But over time, the truth of it could not be denied. Eventually, Bowlby's theory planted the seeds for scientific research over the next fifty years that would prove the importance of parent-infant bonding in creating secure relationships over the lifespan.

Many of us grew up subject to these views of parenting and childrearing. Ben and Claire, along with most couples in marital distress, have no clue how much their current problems are increased by their personal histories of parental bonding and the culture out of which they came.

## Childhood Attachment Styles

How we relate to the people we love when we have needs is called our attachment style. This is the extent to which we allow others to come in close (connect) or push others away (disconnect) when we feel vulnerable. Our attachment styles are established in our first years of life and often stay the same into adulthood. Scientists have learned that attachment styles have a profound effect on our relationships, health, and even leadership success.

Each person's attachment style has a lot to do with his or her need for security in relationships. Being secure in the world and living without fear and anxiety is foundational. Yet we are born into an imperfect world with parents who carry their own deep fears and insecurities about love. Our early experiences with our parents place an imprint on our brains that we carry for the rest of our lives. As a therapist, I believe that the contradiction between the love we were created to live in, and the actual experience of insecure love in our most vital relationships, creates our greatest challenge in life.

Ben and Claire grew up with parents who did not know how to comfort them when they were in emotional distress. Neither of them could rely on their parents for emotional comfort when they needed them the most. They didn't know it growing up, but each developed a particular attachment style—a way of responding to the people around them—because of it.

Mary Ainsworth, a colleague of John Bowlby, devised an experiment that demonstrated how attachment styles are formed and expressed. Ainsworth observed the behaviors of toddlers whose mothers left them alone for a brief time. All of the children showed distress when left alone—but Ainsworth defined the children's attachment styles based on how they were able to receive comfort upon their mother's return. Based on these responses, she placed them into three major attachment categories, which came to be known as *secure, anxious/ambivalent,* and *avoidant* attachment styles. The research of Ainsworth, along with many follow-up studies, have found that the following patterns of behavior of mothers and infants are typical of these attachment styles.

## The Secure Attachment Style

The secure attachment style develops when mothers are responsive to the emotional communications of their infants. They pick them up more quickly when they cry or appear to be in distress. These mothers are more sensitive, accepting, have a high capacity to cooperate with their infants, and are emotionally accessible.

Securely attached infants cry less and are able to handle the stress of separation more easily than insecure children. They are able to be comforted much more quickly after a separation. They seek out more physical comfort and are happy to return it. They tend to express less anger than anxious/ambivalent babies.

These "secure attachment" mothers are better at adjusting their caretaking to their babies' emotional cues. They tend to smile more, offer more happy responses, and make more playful vocalizations. It is interesting to note that the mothers of securely attached infants do not actually spend more time interacting with their children. It is the quality of their interactions that makes the difference. Overall, they are much more loving, tender, and attentive. They rarely distress their children. They give them the love and attention they clearly want, rather than imposing behaviors upon them.

## The Anxious/Ambivalent Attachment Style

Mothers of children with anxious attachment styles are unpredictable. They often shift from anger to passivity, from chaotic behavior to seeming unawareness of their children's needs.

While these mothers express their love through play, delight, or by teaching their infants new skills, they have difficulty loving them in direct response to what their infants are actually asking for. These mothers become more frustrated when their babies are angry or demanding.

Inconsistency of response and a lack of attunement to a child's emotional communications can cause the child to lose trust in the mother. When anxious/ambivalent children are left alone, their mothers have a difficult time convincing their children that they are available to them. These children are overly emotional when afraid. They need extra reassurance to settle down.

## The Avoidant Attachment Style

The mothers of children with avoidant attachment styles are much more rejecting. These mothers show less emotional expression and are less affectionate when holding their babies. They appear to work at containing their anger and irritation. They tend to be rougher in their physical interactions as well.

Mary Main, a colleague of Ainsworth, observed that the mothers of avoidant infants "mocked their infants or spoke sarcastically to them; some stared them down." These mothers often report disliking physical contact with their infants. As a result of this lack of warm, loving contact, these infants show no signs of even *wanting* to be held. They do not snuggle or cling. Their mothers often carry them limply, like sacks of potatoes. They learn early to disconnect from their attachment need and become self-sufficient.

While some of what we describe here may suggest to you an abusive relationship, most often the situation is subtler than that. There are mothers who simply do not connect with their babies, who are uncomfortable with caring for them, and who seem incapable of entering into their children's emotional lives. Of course, the avoidant mother has her own reasons for being that way—remember that mothers had childhoods, too—but the consequences are still very real: these children are likely to face difficult relationship issues as adults.

## Ben and Claire's Attachment Styles

On the surface, both Ben and Claire seemed to have model parents. Their material needs were readily met, and both were adorable in appearance. However, they were both insecurely attached as children; they learned from a young age that they could not count on their parents to be there when they needed them most. These feelings remained inside of them into their adulthood.

Seemingly independent and responsible, Ben had been left alone while the family focused attention on his disabled brother, Max. Ben's mother struggled with a low-level depression that resulted from her upbringing. She had a Dr. Spock hands-off style that made Ben withdraw early from seeking emotional support. He learned as a baby that the only time he got picked up was when he *didn't* cry. Before he'd even reached the age of one, he'd mastered the ability to suppress his emotions if he were to have any hope of getting attention. Ben developed an *avoidant attachment style.*

Understanding this provides great insight into his stoic responses to Claire, and his discomfort and shame over the moment when he'd cried at her discovery of his affair.

As a child, Ben even managed to hide his pain and fear when he fell out of a tree and broke his arm. When he needed love most, he learned to withdraw into his imaginary world. On the outside, independent Ben looked like a model child. He rarely fussed or got into trouble. He knew his marching orders and was determined to work harder and better than his peers.

Growing up, Ben responded to the emotionally cold atmosphere in his home by shutting down his need for emotional comfort. From a very early age, he learned to play alone and remain oblivious to whether or not his parents were in the room. He learned to be self-nurturing and survived by retreating deeply into his internal world. He became very skillful at navigating around his own deepest needs, and learned how to disappear at the hint of emotional conflict. His superior intellect facilitated his mastery over these coping skills. There was always an adult-like quality about Ben that helped him succeed in school and at everything else he tried. He became a Type A high-achiever.

Claire's parents, by contrast, were busy being exemplary church leaders and socialites. Her mother's nurture had been hot and cold. Claire grew up with an *anxious/ambivalent childhood attachment style.*

There was a lack of emotional sensitivity in Claire's generational line that ultimately caused Claire's mother to be emotionally inconsistent in her mothering. At times she was responsive, while at other times she was frustrated and angry. Claire's mother had followed the advice of experts at the time to keep Claire on a schedule and let her cry herself to sleep. Claire's persistent crying during her first year of life was a symptom of her unmet need for emotional comfort.

As a result of her anxious/ambivalent attachment style, Claire grew up extremely sensitive and emotionally insecure. She had learned from a very young age not to trust that her mother would be there when she needed her most. When Claire's mother rocked her crib, it was with her foot; she didn't pick her up when she cried. She seemed to believe that distraction, rather than affection, was the best cure for fear or neediness. This only heightened Claire's insecurity.

As we've stated, Claire's childhood perfectionism was expressed in an attempt to win love and attention from her parents. She hoped that getting good grades on her papers would get her the attention that she so deeply craved. While this strategy often worked, it did not fill the void. From the time she was a child, anxiety and insecurity created a hollow feeling in her gut that no one seemed able to soothe.

This state of being followed Claire into adulthood, marriage, and raising kids. As an adult, Claire continued to try to please others with her excellence, mostly by portraying her marriage and family as ideal. While she was determined that her kids would have what she never had—love and warmth—her behavior toward them sometimes became controlling and stifling. Claire's life was all about performance, about catering to what others perceived, about making sure that her actions showed well publicly.

Somewhere along the line, Ben and Claire—two people with deep connection needs from childhood—found themselves repelling each other because of those very needs.

## Insecure Attachment and Shame

Shame is often a result of children growing up with insecure attachment styles. When their parents do not respond to their needs, they develop a negative view of themselves. They make the assumption that somehow they don't deserve love and attention. This is the root of the emotion of shame. The shame that is formed in childhood often stays with us in adulthood.

Shame is the unspeakable disappointment with self. Shame is fear-based and is usually a reaction to hurt. It causes children to question their integrity or worthiness, and makes us feel bad or wrong about having basic needs and wants. It causes us to feel that we are bad, stupid, or a failure.

Shame is different from guilt. Guilt is remorse about having done something that hurts someone else. Shame is *feeling bad about who we are* rather than about what we have done. Shame can cause a whole range of emotional and relationship problems that impact us for the rest of our lives.

Unfortunately, parents often use shame to change unwanted behavior. They may induce shame by using degrading statements such as, "you bad girl," "shame on you," "you selfish brat," "big boys don't cry," "you are impossible," "you are stupid," or even "you are ugly." Many have been shamed with questions such as, "What is wrong with you?" or "Why can't you act like so-and-so?" Parents who drive their children to meet high standards often manipulate them with shame. They can also induce shame by withdrawing affection or adopting looks of contempt or demeaning tones of voice. Criticism, teasing, and embarrassing forms of discipline are shame inducing.

Shame is a common way of channeling parental anger and frustration. Parents who struggle with their own shame issues are more likely to make children feel ashamed when they are displeased with their behavior. Attempts to use shame to get children to work harder usually backfire, as shame has been shown to decrease motivation and initiative.

Shame damages trust in self and others. The feeling of being unworthy, unlovable, or "not enough" can cause us to question our competence. It also causes us to doubt that others will trust or be there for us when we need them most. It feels as if there is no one to turn to when we are overtaken by shame, that we are defective and must hide our shameful selves from others.

In Daniel Goleman's book, *Emotional Intelligence,* he suggests that shame causes relationship difficulties and violent behavior.[11] Researcher Brené Brown has connected shame with depression, low self-esteem, and violence. She believes shame damages the foundation from which love grows.

Shame pierces the heart of the fragile child's self-confidence. Children do not have enough life experience to evaluate themselves within the context of the larger world. They trust their parents to help them define who they are and make them feel competent and lovable. When parents use shame, the child turns against himself. He becomes paralyzed with defective and deficient feelings. He does not learn how to grow in proficiency by learning from experience.

But perhaps the most tragic outcome of shame is that it robs us of our basic capacity to live joyfully. Fearing the judgment of others causes a restraint of self-expression. There is a paralyzing self-consciousness that paints over the whimsy of our creative behavior. This causes us to monitor our words and behaviors too closely, which in turn dampens our capacity to feel alive in the moment. *Shame inhibits the expression of all emotions except anger.*

Transparency and empathy, the foundation of intimate relationships, become difficult once shame enters the equation. Ben and Claire grew up paralyzed by shame from the time they were young. It interfered with their capacity to identify and accept their emotional needs. They did not know what a mutually satisfying love relationship looked like. In dating, Claire found herself bending toward the needs of others and Ben found himself overwhelmed and fleeing when relationships felt dependent. Shame kept both of them from owning the truth of what they needed in love relationships.

People who struggle with shame often move from aggression to silent withdrawal. When shame is activated, they are more likely to engage in passive-aggressive behavior. This was true for Ben, who withdrew from close relationships when his shame was activated. He covered his shame by using contempt, superiority, and domineering behaviors.

Claire manifested her shame with obsessive perfectionism. She held herself to standards that only God could attain. This kept her in a position of feeling perpetually unworthy and angry with herself. Her genuine accomplishments were never celebrated. In her mind, if she was capable of achieving it, then it must not be important or worthy of celebration.

## Childhood Trust

Trust is a birthright. It is the natural state of being for little ones undamaged by the harshness of life. While children are naturally self-centered, they have a beautiful capacity to love and trust. Unless frightened, they bond with ease and more than return all the love that is poured into them. They are pre-wired to trust. Psychologist Erik Erikson has pointed out that trust is the foundation for realistic hope in future relationships.[12]

There are genetic problems that affect some children's capacity to receive and express love. The autism spectrum disorders come to mind. But, in most cases, it is what is done to children that causes them to lack trust. Mistrust is engendered by behavior more often than by genetics.

Fear is the enemy of trust. Bonding with others is our greatest asset for growth and survival, but when those we bond with betray us, we stop trusting. When we begin to fear the person we once trusted the most, the whole world seems like a scary place. We question ourselves and our judgment, and are careful to not let ourselves be vulnerable in the future.

We trust those who lovingly help us understand ourselves. This is especially true for children, who have everything to learn about why they feel and behave the way they do. Their brains rely on the feedback of adults. When the adults they trust do not provide compassionate communication, they stop reaching for connection. Their trust has been broken.

The key to their survival as a couple would be for them to find the secure connection that had eluded them in their close relationships all of their lives.

part four
# new love

Attraction's Fantasy and
the Chemistry of New Love

STORY

# The Feeling
# of Paradise

*Every heart sings a song, incomplete, until another
heart whispers back. Those who wish to sing always find
a song. At the touch of a lover, everyone becomes a poet.*
—Plato

The day had been exhausting for Ben.

All the emotions bouncing around in their therapy session were more difficult and tiring to process than he had imagined. But it did seem as if he and Claire were making headway. In their brief moments together after the session, Claire had seemed less frantic. She had stopped yelling at him—at least for now. The therapy seemed to be calming her down, and Ben was grateful for that. Still, he had left the session wondering if it was all necessary, if there wasn't an easier way. He would end things with Bridgette. He longed to get past this and get on with life . . . the kids, his job, and Claire. He'd moved beyond making excuses. He regretted his betrayal.

But in the quiet of his own thoughts, Ben could hear Bridgette's compelling "come-hither" voice competing with that of his wife. *Gosh, I miss that woman.* This emotional memory triggered his primal desire to escape. *Do I really even want to preserve my life with Claire?* Ben's mind was cluttered with unanswerable questions, doubts, confusion, and fear.

The best thing that had happened all day was that Claire's mom had called to cancel the evening visit. She had twisted her ankle on her afternoon walk and, though it didn't seem serious, she needed to keep it elevated and iced. She apologized profusely and promised a visit, "maybe with Dad," sometime during the weekend. It was all Ben could do to keep from dancing with joy. *There is a God.*

Ben felt like celebrating the end of a difficult day. An over-booked roster of patients, the difficult therapy session and the kids' school program had drained him. He reached into the wine fridge for a bottle of Chardonnay, pulled the cork loose, and filled his glass. Relieved that Claire was preoccupied with the kids, he relished his evening privacy even more than usual. Slipping off his clothes with the day's troubles, he climbed into a steaming hot tub and sank into oblivion.

Claire was on autopilot as she presided over the kids' dinner, homework, baths, and bedtime. She, too, was relieved that her mom had been a no-show. While she longed for her mom's comfort, she couldn't possibly have divulged what was going on—and skirting the issue all evening would have been exhausting. Claire had just enough energy left to listen to Leslie read while Jake navigated through cyber galaxies on his tablet.

Claire finally tucked the kids in, deposited sweet kisses on their cheeks, and quietly closed their doors. The warmth of Leslie's "I love you, Mommy" followed her down the hall to the master suite.

Claire brushed out her curls and stepped into her silk PJs, ending her day curled in the chair that perfectly enveloped her petite frame. She grabbed a book and pulled out the photo that doubled as a bookmark, then rested her head on the softness of the cushion. She stared at the black-and-white of Ben until the image blurred through her tears. Falling into sleep, her memories became dreams.

As Ben's head hit the pillow, he began to take inventory of the day's events and those of the last ten years. And Bridgette. Thoughts of her filled the empty spaces in his mind—so much so that he was afraid. He wondered if he could really let go of a relationship that had filled the gaps that had developed between him and Claire.

Restless, Ben sat up in bed and grabbed the latest issue of the *Journal of Pediatric Medicine,* hoping to replace his dangerous thoughts with more productive ones. *I know I can save a kid's life. My relationship? That I'm not so sure about.*

Claire woke up the next morning thinking about the evening ahead—a girls' night out with her sister and friends—and she was strangely nervous about it. Steph had suggested it earlier that week: "It'll be good for you to get out and have some fun. Why not join me and my girlfriends?"

"Steph, what are you wearing tonight? This seems so strange, going out on the town without my husband," she said in an early morning call.

"Claire, we're not going out on the town," Steph reminded her. "We're going for a couple of drinks and appetizers at the Blue Room. It's not like we're clubbing. It will be fun, you'll see."

"Fine. Do you think my new black dress is too much? I kind of bought it with Ben in mind. He loves me in black, you know."

"This isn't a big deal, sis. Wear whatever's comfortable … as long as it's not jeans and a tee shirt. And lose the ponytail. This is a nice place."

"What? Ben used to love my ponytail. He thought it made me sexy-cute. That's who I was when he fell in love with me. Geez, what happened to us? We were crazy about each other."

"Yeah, yeah, don't get all mushy again, Claire. We're not thinking about Ben tonight. You deserve a break. I gotta go now. I'll see you at six."

Ben felt agitated as he waited for his first patient of the day. He couldn't shake the thought of Claire going out with the girls that night, something she hadn't done since they'd had kids. *Is this what wives do when their husbands work late? Is she trying to make me jealous or get back at me?* It seemed a bit odd, but he convinced himself to stay away from suspicion or accusations. The slight pang of jealousy he felt was a foreign sensation.

Ben recalled their first meeting. Gosh, she really was sexy back then with her cute blonde ponytail bouncing against her shoulders. She had made him feel so important—like the special love of her life. What happened? She changed so much after those first couple of years.

Unlike Claire, Ben hadn't hung out with the popular kids in high school. He had stayed focused on running track and keeping up his 4.5 GPA. The choices he'd made were all focused on his college apps and what would bolster his odds of going to an Ivy League school. There had been a girl named Tyra who had gotten Ben off track—he wasn't proud of his one-night stand with her. While Ben and Claire had come "close" several times, they'd never actually "gone all the way" before marrying. Claire had always resented that she wasn't Ben's first, and didn't hesitate to bring it up once in a while.

*Tyra was a beautiful senior when Ben was just a sophomore. She had had a bit of a rough life, left pretty much alone by her divorced parents to fend for herself. She was certainly not the type of girl Ben tended to date, but her come-ons were hard to resist. When she knocked on the front door of his parent's suburban Chicago home wearing a tight-fitting, low-cut tee, Ben's blood pressure surged. She entreated him to take her to the prom (a ploy to make another boy jealous, he found out later) and he found himself saying yes. The fact that his parents disapproved quite vocally was added incentive: Ben was sick and tired of always being the perfect kid.*

*At the dance, it was nice holding Tyra close while slow dancing. Her slinky, satiny gown revealed every bit of woman in her. Something in Ben came alive for the first time ever and he liked the feeling.*

*Tyra had come prepared—her gaudy leatherette clutch held a full flask and she quickly got Ben tipsy. They left early and took a drive down to the river to watch the stars. That's what everyone did on prom night; why should he be any different? Needless to say…one thing led to another.*

*That was it. One time.*

*Though Tyra made it clear she wanted to continue seeing him, Ben never went out with her again. At one point, she alluded to a positive pregnancy test, but Ben wouldn't take the bait. He may have been naïve but he wasn't stupid, and he'd heard through the grapevine that she'd used that ploy before.*

That was so long ago.

*Why am I thinking about that now?*

Though Tyra hadn't been his type, he'd loved the euphoric feeling she'd inspired in him. Which brought him right back to Bridgette. He flushed a bit as he imagined a physical encounter with her.

*Stop it, Ben. You cannot go there, even in your fantasies. Tyra, Claire, Bridgette—what an evolution. What am I thinking? This is not evolution. It ends with Claire. Bridgette cannot be in the picture. Not the permanent picture, anyway. What I have, or had, with Bridgette must end. I have to find a way back to loving or at least being content with Claire. It's too painful otherwise.*

At first, Claire had rocked Ben's world. She was beautiful, intelligent without needing to show it off. She had a heartbreaking smile.

*She really did intoxicate me.*

He'd focused on finding ways to win her affections. She'd sent mixed signals, making him feel as if she was off limits while pulling him toward her at the same time.

As they got to know each other, he found himself racing over to her dorm room each day after class. They'd leave the door ajar according to the rules, but her seductive gaze would lure him quickly into her arms. It took every bit of restraint they could muster not to cross lines. Unlike Tyra, there was nothing cheap about Claire.

What had happened since those days? Thinking about it, Ben could feel the excitement of those relationships. He could remember the heat and deep connection. Now…things were different.

During their courtship, Ben and Claire had spent lots of time together. Talk of marriage came up early and often. When Claire was in Ben's arms, he was all in. But Claire was a planner, and the more she pressed him to take things to the next level, it was like a light switch went off inside of Ben. He lost his fire.

*She constantly questioned my love and intentions. Yikes, some things don't change. I guess she's always seemed a little insecure when it comes to our relationship. Should I have run from all that when I had the chance?*

But Ben hadn't run. He had made that vow with Claire, for better or worse. Why had he committed to her? Was it the promise of their early erotic attraction, or his sense that she was part of his life plan? Maybe both.

So, now, everything was a mess. How would he right this wrong? He knew the answer: Whatever feelings he had for Bridgette must cease to exist. He was torn now, between commitment and what seemed like a new and exciting love. He couldn't do it though; he had to stay true to his vows. Ben wondered how Claire was able to continue to have faith in a love that felt a million miles away and many years ago. He would have to find the same determination.

The Blue Room was alive with an eclectic after-work crowd. Claire froze at the picture before her. She and Ben had never been there. He was more into subtle settings. The Blue Room sparkled with more excitement than he could handle.

*He's become a bit of a drip. All work, no fun anymore.*

Claire's wide eyes locked onto her sister's. Steph motioned her toward a pub-style table in the thick of it all. "Oh my gosh, this is a bit crazy, isn't it?" she said, exchanging hugs with the other women in turn and then pulling herself up onto a stool at the high top. She needed a glass of wine to take the edge off. Reading her mind, the waitress appeared with an appetizer menu and a long list of specialty drinks.

"A glass of the house merlot for now, please. I need a minute to look at the food menu."

The others followed Claire's lead and studied the mouth-watering selections. Claire began to relax and enjoy the setting the minute she'd taken the first sip of wine. The women chatted like schoolgirls, somewhat oblivious to the boisterous crowd surrounding them. "Wow, I haven't felt this good in weeks," Claire said. "Not sure if it's the wine or the great company."

"It's the wine," said the others in unison, chuckling.

Claire felt a nudge but chalked it up to the crowded conditions.

She didn't realize the gesture had been intentional until her sister nodded toward a handsome guy behind her chair. Taking a quick glance over her shoulder, Claire recognized a familiar and friendly face.

"Mike, is that you? Mike Havard? It's been forever." Claire flushed, certain that the smile she'd flashed at her old high-school beau was inappropriately wide.

Her adolescent crush flashed before her. Actually, it had been more than a crush. Claire had been in love with Mike, and at the time, she'd thought he loved her back, even when he didn't show it. His behavior had alternated between hot and cold, on and off, like a faucet. This had only encouraged her to try harder to land him—just as she had chased a lot of other potential suitors. And Claire had had her ways, her own kind of seduction designed to lure them in. While she'd remained technically chaste, she had used her sexuality to attract guys—especially those who were fickle or indifferent.

Love had always seemed a bit mysterious to Claire. She'd often felt lonely, whether she was dating or not. She'd never liked it when her boyfriends talked to other girls, but she'd laughed it off and feigned a sense of security she didn't possess. *Was that how love was supposed to feel?*

In the early days, Claire had felt that Ben, too, would abandon her. Today, she was feeling the overwhelming fear of abandonment all over again.

"Hey Claire, how about an introduction?" said one of her friends—the unattached one. Before Claire could say anything, she reached past her toward Mike and said, "Hi, I'm Lindsey. Claire and I have been friends for ages."

But it was soon clear that Mike had no interest in Claire's friend. His eyes were glued to Claire and he looked smitten all over again. Claire took another long swallow of her wine. *What* the heck, he's an old high-school friend. Between the wine and his flattery, she felt a glimmer of self-confidence—and it felt pretty good.

Claire's sister and girlfriends soon blurred into the background as she and Mike spent the next forty-five minutes catching up. Claire's schoolgirl giddiness drew Mike in closer. Claire felt warm and tingly, even as she talked about Ben, her kids, and her love for photography.

*What's going on here? I'm happily married. Well, I'm* married *anyway.*

Claire excused herself and made her way to the ladies room. She pulled an H2O mister from her bag and spritzed her face without disturbing her makeup. She carefully applied a fresh coat of lipstick. After all, she didn't want to look frumpy for an old flame. She knew without a shadow of doubt that he wouldn't get near those lips, but he would be looking. Claire steadied herself. *I could get even with Ben. He certainly deserves it.* Everything in Claire's body, including her fluttering heart, said, *Go get Mike.* But her ten years of marriage and deep commitment to her family put her brakes on. *Ben may have less discretion and fewer morals, but I'll be damned if I stoop to that level.*

Claire gave her face another good spritz, patted off the excess lipstick, and returned to her friends. When she saw no sign of Mike, she suspected that her sister—who always had her best interests in mind—had sent him packing. Claire was sobered by the thought of her potential misstep, that she'd even contemplated being unfaithful. She was alarmed by how easy it could be to make a choice that could ruin a long-term marriage. *Had Ben fallen prey to the same warm flush and fluttering that I just did? Well, maybe, but he didn't have the decency, guts, or scruples to say no. Of course...if it weren't for Steph, maybe I wouldn't have either.*

They met at a quiet café in a discreet neighborhood.

Ben had his guard up, knowing just how vulnerable he was. Bridgette always had a magical effect on him, and he knew she wouldn't make this easy. Her emerald-colored silk dress clung to her in all the right places. She looked alluringly delicious, as always.

Ben had gotten them a quiet table in the corner. His tentative reach for Bridgette's hand warmed them both. "Bridgette, this has been . . . you have been great. And you know how much I . . ." Ben's tongue thickened as he fought for the words. "You know how much I care about you. Our relationship has meant more to me than you can know. But I can't live this kind of life. The kids need me. We've got to stop this."

Bridgette's grasp tightened with his every word. "Oh Ben, at one level I totally get it. At another, well, I just don't know how I can let you go." She swept her auburn locks from her eyes, uncovering their passion.

Ben melted. He had second thoughts about everything he had come here to say. Could he really end this incredibly consuming relationship for a stale and painful one with Claire? He had never felt more conflicted. *Can I really do this?* He knew he didn't have a choice.

A voice behind him made Ben freeze. He released Bridgette's hand. Startled and five shades of red, he stood and reached out his sweaty palm to shake the hand of his colleague. His careful planning had backfired. He had been seen with another woman in a romantic, out-of-the-way café. To make matters worse, the colleague's wife was a friend of Claire's.

Ben attempted to stand tall and strong, but inside, he felt the size of a child.

Claire and her sister took taxis home. The house was quiet when Claire tiptoed in. Had Ben's meeting run late? On her way to the bedroom, she saw him sitting in his dimly lit study. She wasn't ready to talk to him. She certainly couldn't tell him about getting a little tipsy and flirting with her high-school flame. *I didn't do anything wrong. Or did I?* She would wrestle with that over the next few days. If they were to have an honest relationship, could she with a clear conscience keep this from him?

*Oh God, this is so hard. Why can't we just go back to those early days?*

In the quiet of his study, Ben had begun his own sort of wrestling. *What have I done? To Bridgette? To Claire?* Ben sunk deep into his chair. *I'm not sure that I deserve either of them.* He felt smothered by guilt and fear. He had no idea how he would dig himself out of this hole. How long would it be before word got out about his evening with Bridgette? Would he confess yet another misstep to Claire? Or would he walk on eggshells, hoping his colleague would keep quiet? Had the man's look been one of sympathy or disgust?

Ben couldn't bring himself to get in bed with Claire.

And Claire was relieved.

10

THERAPY

# Uncovering Aloneness and Addiction

*The thing that I'm most worried about is just being alone
without anybody to care for or someone who will care for me.*
—Anne Hathaway

A s I prepared for my next session, I wondered what I was in for. The wounds that Ben and Claire have inflicted on each other are fresh. I anticipated more cries and attacks.

As with most couples at this stage, emotional communication is still a foreign language to each of them.

Claire is quick to express her pain and protest, and just as quick to cut Ben when he doesn't get her. He cuts her just as deeply, sometimes with painful sarcasm but most often with aloof indifference. It is the latter that seems innocent to Ben but rips the widest hole in Claire's heart. It signals to her that he could walk away at any moment and not look back.

I began our session with my normal test of the temperature of the relationship. "How are you each feeling about your relationship this week?

Ben responded first, saying that the two of them had not argued as much.

Without acknowledging that, Claire mentioned that, "as usual," Ben had been working constantly, often late into the evenings.

Drilling in more deeply, I suggested to Ben that his aloofness was a trigger for Claire, leaving her wondering where he was and who he was with. He admitted still not fully realizing how that affected her. I felt his response was genuine.

I suggested that this might have been a pattern over the years...

**Therapist:** Okay. So your communication has been dying over the years because you shut down or fight when you need each other the most. Claire, you have learned to keep your hurt to yourself as much as possible. Then Ben tries to talk to you and you explode with anger.

**Claire:** He has been ignoring me for years. I just can't stand it!

**Therapist:** So the loneliness inside of you gets hard to bear. Even though both of you keep extremely busy, it doesn't cover how much it hurts to feel alone. How about you, Ben? What are you feeling when Claire talks about how much she has missed connecting with you?

**Ben:** Well, I have been lonely, too. We hardly ever make love anymore. I have just stopped asking. I wait for the stars to align for a chance to get close. I think she likes spending time with her sister more than she does with me.

**Therapist:** So your love life, in addition to your communication, has felt kind of empty. Tell me more about that. What was lovemaking like early in your relationship?

**Ben:** *(Blushing)* It was fantastic! Of course, we didn't actually have sex before we were married. But we did pretty much everything else. Claire was the most responsive woman that I had been with.

**Claire:** I agree that our lovemaking was great. I didn't say too much about it, but I had some mixed feelings about how far we did go before we got married. I enjoyed it and knew that Ben did as well.

**Therapist:** So, sexual intimacy came very naturally and you were highly aroused by each other. There were some mixed feelings on your part, Claire, but you had no doubt that Ben fulfilled you, and you wanted to do the same for him. What happened in the years after you got married?

**Ben:** It was great for the first couple of years and then it felt like she just kind of cooled off. She just wasn't as responsive or as much fun.

**Claire:** I wasn't as much fun? I was pregnant with Jake! Besides, once you hit med school, you were like the walking dead when you came home. Sure, you would party with the other med students. But you stopped seeing me and loving us.

**Therapist:** So for you, Claire, it felt like you were on the outside of this consuming force that sucked the life right out of Ben. What was that like for you?

**Claire:** It was horrible. I felt lonely and unattractive. I knew that what he was doing was important and that I needed to make the sacrifice. I thought that when we got through med school and had the baby I would get him back. I never did.

**Therapist:** So the disconnect started really early, just a couple of years after you were married. This is such a critical time for couples. The new love chemistry that lights passion up begins to fade at around the two-year mark. It is at this time that attachment insecurities from childhood begin to surface. Claire, you were feeling the need to go deeper with Ben and to have your unmet attachment needs met. Ben, you felt the pull to override your unmet needs and succeed no matter what. To follow in your father's footsteps.

**Ben:** It felt like I had no option. The pressure was overwhelming. It's true I am competitive. But I had no idea how demanding medical school would be. It was like drinking out of a fire hose.

**Therapist:** So, for you, Ben, probably for the first time in your life, there was this fear of failure. That if you didn't give it everything you had, you could let Claire and your family down. It felt like you were fighting for survival.

**Ben:** Survival is right. I had peers that were washing out of the program, and they weren't stupid. It was survival of the fittest.

**Therapist:** This was such an incredibly stressful and vulnerable time for each of you. Being married opened up even deeper needs for connection in you, Claire. Marriage triggered the burden of responsibility for you, Ben, and all of the fears that you would not measure up.

**Ben and Claire:** *(Both acknowledge with nods and facial discomfort that I am touching some very old injuries)*

There are certain points in therapy sessions when it seems there is a breakthrough, or perhaps something short of that but yet significant—a simple agreement on a simple thing. This was one such moment, as Claire and Ben accepted not only their own hurt, but each other's.

I continued down this track, exploring the hurt one had caused the other, and getting each of them to identify the specific emotions they had experienced. This was the beginning of a big step forward.

⊶⊷

**Therapist:** Ben, what is happening to you as you hear about how deeply Claire has been injured?

**Ben:** I feel terrible. I had no intention of injuring her. Bridgette understood the pressures of my work. I didn't feel Claire understood them in the same way. But, believe me, I never intended for the thing with Bridgette to go as far as it did.

**Claire:** You never gave me the chance to understand!

**Therapist:** So, Ben, you are feeling horrible about how Claire is suffering. You had no idea how talking about your feelings to Bridgette could trigger such powerful emotions in your wife. How did this relationship with Bridgette happen?

**Ben:** I don't know. It started out as just a friendship. We worked together and talked about cases. At some point, we started opening up about our personal lives. I didn't even realize what was happening. Even then, the emotions that were opened up in me were overwhelming. I began to feel things that I had not felt since the first year of my relationship with Claire. I didn't know I could feel that way. I never wanted to leave Claire. I never stopped loving Claire. I had just been so emotionally shut down, and this relationship activated feelings that seemed beyond my control.

**Claire:** I trusted you. I never doubted that you would do the right thing. Everyone, including my family, put you on such a high pedestal. I don't know that I can look at you the same way again.

**Ben:** (Nods, seemingly close to tears)

**Therapist:** Okay, let me try to summarize some things. I know this is difficult to understand, for each of you.

Claire, you feel devastated. It is frightening to see an emotional part of Ben, one you have always craved for yourself, emerge out of nowhere. You saw this part of him early in your relationship, but then just let go of longing for him in that way. You trusted that he would do the right thing. That he would be a reliable partner who would never betray you. To hear that another woman could have this kind of effect on him has shaken you deeply.

Even though Ben says that he never stopped loving you, it feels impossible right now to believe him. You feel that because someone else had such a powerful emotional effect on him, that you have lost what is sacred between the two of you forever.

Ben, you feel shame and confusion that your emotions could take you over this way. You never stopped wanting to be with Claire and to build a life with her, but the intense feelings you felt in courtship and the first years of marriage subsided over time. Suddenly, those emotional and sexual feelings were tapped by this new relationship. They took you over. You found yourself saying and doing things that you didn't think you were capable of. This is the power that a new relationship can have over any of us at any stage of life, regardless of how committed we are to our current one.

Nothing I'm saying absolves you of responsibility for your actions with Bridgette. Nor am I absolving you, Claire—notwithstanding this hurtful thing that Ben has done—for your own responsibility in what has happened in your relationship with Ben. We'll talk more about your role in these events later.

Can the two of you hear these words from me right now and accept at least some portion of the truth I'm speaking?

**Ben:** Yes.

**Claire:** *(Reluctantly nods)*

**Therapist:** Good. . . . Now, I want to offer you something else, something that has been a reality you both have been dealing with, yet neither of you have been aware of.

I want to talk with you for a few minutes about "new love" and "mature love," and how the difference between them is something you two may not understand. I believe the assumptions about love that you brought into marriage have left you somewhat defense-less and led you to where you are now.

## SCIENCE

# Attached or Addicted to New Love

*Being out of control and too "high" on love*
*can be as destructive as an addiction to alcohol,*
*drugs, food or shopping.*
— Dr. Judy Kuriansky

As children become adolescents and move toward young adulthood, there is nothing more captivating, exciting, and enticing than the experience of new love. All of us can relate to that first adolescent experience of having the "hots" for someone. The heart-pounding, overwhelming feelings produced by just seeing this person across the school grounds made all other types of excitement pale in comparison.

Like most of us, Ben and Claire were initially sucked into the vortex of attraction. The rush of feelings and fantasies of fulfilled dreams were dizzying to their senses. The attraction was automatic. They both felt a rush of electricity flow through them, drawing them to connect. They pursued each other with focus and excitement.

The cocktail of physical attraction, personality, and position was like a drug that signaled each of their brains that they had found what their hearts had been longing for. Once they latched on, there was no letting go. They would begin the dance of new love and stay at it until they had either attached for life or concluded that this was not a heart's desire after all.

Understanding the chemistry of new love is critical. So many hearts are broken and marriages destroyed when people do not understand the difference between new and mature love. Every one of us can recall a time in our lives when new love had its hold on us. More songs and poems have been penned about new love than any other subject. As single adults, we spend more time thinking about, fretting about, and pursuing new love than we care to admit. Desire for it motivates us to make heroic efforts in order to attract the attention of our desire's object. For single and available adults, new love is nothing short of magical.

After we are married, it's a different story: New love in that context can destroy our lives. The biological and spiritual purpose of new love is to ignite our rocket engines so we can defy the gravity that keeps us to ourselves. It inspires us to overcome our inhibitions and propels us toward the other person at the speed of light. It goads us into seductive behaviors such as flirting, sexual banter, and the overwhelming need for physical touch. These things can distract even the most committed people from their marriages. New love is full of big emotions—but it is also a predictable, biologically programmed drive. It has the power to destroy what we have spent a lifetime loving and sacrificing our lives for.

## New Love Chemistry

Ben had remained committed to his marital vows for ten years. Thoughts of infidelity were not even an issue. So, why did he fall under the spell of new love with Bridgette, at the expense of his wife's trust? What was so powerful in this liaison that it caused him to lose control and put his marriage and family in jeopardy?

Neuroscientists Larry Young and Brian Alexander suggest that new love is an addiction. When people are under the influence of a powerful drug, they will do just about anything to get more of it, often destroying the relationships that matter most to them. So, what is the drug that makes new love so addictive?

Meet the brain chemical known as *dopamine*. It is important to understand that dopamine is essential to our lives—in the right balance. Dopamine depletion is associated with Parkinson's disease. Chronic dopamine over-activity is associated with schizophrenia. Too little dopamine can cause involuntary tremors, and too much can make us crazy to the point of losing touch with reality.

The power of dopamine to affect mood and motivate behavior is profound. Rats will turn down food and water to get more of it. Humans will do just about anything to stay under its spell.

Dopamine makes us "dopey" when it comes to love. Pour a little dopamine "lighter fluid" on the dry kindling of a marriage that has become too busy for time in the bedroom, and the right spark can easily ignite a fire that can burn out of control.

Biological anthropologist Helen Fischer has done extensive research on how different kinds of love produce different neurochemistry and activate different brain structures. Using powerful imaging technology, researchers are able to look at specific activity inside the brain as subjects are shown pictures of people they have feelings for.[13] Fischer's research has demonstrated that new or erotic relationships produce different chemistry and activate different parts of the brain than mature attached relationships.

The novelty and intrigue associated with new and erotic relationships stimulates dopamine, the most powerful reward neurochemical present in man and beast. Dopamine is required to stimulate the pleasure center of the brain, called the *nucleus accumbens*.

To study the phenomenon, scientists hooked laboratory mice up to electrodes that stimulated their brain's pleasure centers. By pressing a lever, the mice would get the same kind of feeling as from sex or addictive drugs. Needless to say, they loved it. They loved it so much that they could not focus on anything else, including their own survival. They would ignore food and water and continue to stimulate themselves to a point of physical collapse.

Researchers have associated the obsessive euphoria that people feel when stimulated by dopamine with the effects of cocaine. This makes perfect sense. Use of cocaine stimulates dopamine release, which activates the nucleus accumbens pleasure center of the brain.

## Dopamine vs. Attachment Dating

Even if we wanted to, we couldn't escape the powerful effect of dopamine when we open ourselves to a new love relationship. No matter how old we are, we feel like goofy teenagers when we are under its intoxicating influence. We become more romantic, buying flowers, composing poems, and making plans for exotic nights out (and in). New-love dopamine-driven relationships elevate sexiness to a new level. Men and women alike can't get enough of the romantic talk and kissing and touching that keep the stream of dopamine flowing.

Yes, each new relationship is special—but what they all have in common is that we enter them under the influence of dopamine's power. It's a primary factor as early as the first date. So, what separates "dopamine dating" from "attachment dating"?

When we understand that dating under the influence of dopamine may cause disastrous errors in judgment, we become cautious about allowing it to motivate important decisions. We can slow down dopamine production by touching less and talking more. We can make a decision to really get to know the person we are dating by being with them in different social settings and at family gatherings. We can seek to understand their values and vision for a fulfilled life. We can spread out the dating process over at least a one-year period in order to get to know them during important life events. All of these strategies can help us regulate how much we allow the new-love feelings that dopamine produces to influence the promises we are making.

It is the promises of love, not the drug high, which deepens and solidifies attachment. It is when we securely attach that we begin to allow our psychology and biology to be profoundly influenced by one other special person whom we hold most dear. No other relationship will influence our lives more than the one with the person to whom we choose to attach.

Understanding the difference between dating for dopamine and dating for attachment is critical for lifelong health and happiness. Dating for dopamine, whether intentional or not, is about using another person as a mood-altering drug. When one is "addicted to love" while at the same time racing down the track into a lifelong relationship, the results can be disastrous. A marriage that comes from such a situation can be disastrous.

When the excitement of new love inevitably wears off and the brain stops delivering mega doses of dopamine, it can be easy to question whether the relationship is the right fit after all. Casting it off and following the dopamine dating trail once again places us back in a vicious cycle. It won't be long before some new love object starts the intoxicating music again—perhaps this is the one? The results are all too predictable.

Clearly, Ben's friendship with Bridgette triggered the dopamine rush he didn't even realize he'd been missing. It's also what happened momentarily to Claire in the restaurant, when she re-encountered an old flame.

I have worked with many middle-aged serial "dopamine

daters" who have ultimately found themselves in a state of devastating self-doubt. They are alone and out of sync with their
attached friends, wondering why a healthy and happy lifelong
partnership keeps eluding them.

I have also counseled many couples who have let the fire in
their marriages die. When they hit middle age, or much earlier,
and begin to wonder if they are still desirable, they often find
themselves lowering their boundaries with the opposite sex. The
newfound excitement they experience in encounters outside of
marriage is fueled by that new-love neurochemistry still lurking inside of them. The powerful dopamine hit makes them feel
young, single, and on the prowl.

While he wasn't looking for a new relationship, Ben none-
theless succumbed to his own chemistry and found himself in
a dangerous situation. When we are not securely attached in
marriage, we become an open target for the power that dopa-
mine-induced love has over us.

Like a cocaine addict wanting to protect his fix at any cost, the
"dopamine-driven betrayer" justifies his behavior, idealizes his
new relationship, and begins to demonize his current life partner.

Building a relationship on attachment sets love in order. Its
foundation is more solid and permanent, less dependent on chemistry. Attachment is about forming a lifelong, mutually fulfilling
partnership. Its goal is lifelong connection rather than temporary
new-love feelings. Attachment allows new lovers to lower their
defenses. It invites the honest sharing of limitations. It builds
enduring trust within a responsive reliable relationship.

The traditional notion that it is unwise to have sex before
marriage is part of the strategy of attachment dating. While this is
not a popular mindset today, we believe that sex in new-love relationships is such a powerful dopamine stimulator that it can cloud
judgment. This can lead to disastrous decisions. Couples not able

to discern the effects of dopamine may find themselves making relationship and life choices they will regret.

Attachment dating is about keeping the relationship secure and growing for the future. Couples who practice attachment dating talk about their physical relationship and actively choose to restrain the heat. They understand that overdosing on passion can cloud their judgment. They work to protect each other from the overwhelming feelings of the dopamine brain bath. Their goal is to deepen their communication and compassionately talk through every problem that might trigger a disconnection. As they learn how to connect and work through differences, they will develop the emotional resiliency necessary to face the challenges that life will bring. Couples who have emotionally secure brains are able to support each other through the storms of life.

## Adolescent Brain

Claire's adolescent years were overflowing with social connections. She was a firecracker burning at both ends as she organized high school and college events, each one more extraordinary than the last. She thrived in her self-appointed role of social chairwoman. She finally found the attention she had not gotten from her mother by organizing successful church functions.

Ben was much less social than Claire. Though he wasn't all that comfortable around girls, he and his buddies did feed their imaginations by gluing themselves to the pages of porn magazines.

Claire's flirtatiousness with Ben stirred things in him that could not be contained. Once she'd attracted his attention, she fanned the flames vigorously throughout their early dating years.

From ages twelve to twenty-four, the adolescent brain is driven by powerful chemistry. This influences the way we think, remember, reason, and make decisions. It is during this time that we have the most courage for being energetic and creative. The power burst we experience throughout these years directs our lives in ways that will profoundly shape our futures.

In his book on the teenage brain, Dan Siegel suggests that adolescents exhibit four drives: *novelty seeking, social engagement, increased emotional intensity, and creative explora*tion. Each of these heightened behaviors has a profound influence on all relationships. Interactions with parents and peers alike are strongly affected by the intensity of heightened hormonal adolescent behaviors.

For adolescents, new is nearly always better. "Creative" is valued more highly than "sameness." Emotional intensity is craved, and fed by such activities as extreme sports. And all of this is played out among peers; it is a period of active social engagement. Adolescent brains offer a reward for trying new things that almost automatically lead away from anything not the latest and greatest. The drive toward novelty makes a whole lot of parental behaviors and preferences appear boring and even stupid. Likewise, adolescent brain chemistry drives youngsters to value social engagement above family ties.

What appears to be contrary behavior is not simply rebellion or hatred of the parents who have sacrificed life and limb for their kids' existence. This behavior—whether it is wearing bizarre fashions, bungee jumping, or devouring alternative music—is driven by dopamine.

When it comes to romantic relationships, the four gears of adolescence, combined with the dopamine, creates a one-two punch that can be volatile in the extreme. The intensity that adolescents feel in their love relationships cannot be underestimated. What adults call "puppy love" is more like a complete mind and body takeover. Adolescents become consumed by thoughts and feelings for the latest object of their affection.

These early adolescent-brain experiences have everything

to do with attachment needs, wants, and hurts. They shape the attachment styles of a person for a lifetime. The pain of lost love, regardless of how frivolous it may seem to the adult observer, creates a powerful memory imprint that will never be forgotten. It is the sum of these love experiences that shapes how secure or insecure we will be in forming lifelong attachment bonds.

The attachment style that adolescents bring to relationships either helps them or makes it more difficult for them to navigate relationship challenges. Claire's anxious attachment style encouraged her to throw herself at every new and exciting boy who crossed her path. Her personal brand of easy seduction was a shiny lure that she would cast in the direction of anyone who caught her eye.

And catch them she did. In her day, Claire reeled in a number of guys that she should have thrown back. Her insecure need for love and attention made it difficult for her to evaluate whether the boys she was attracting had the attachment security to love her in the careful consistent way that she needed.

Once they were seduced by her charms, she was quick to pull them out of circulation and do everything in her power to get them to love only her. Her sexual wiles were too powerful for most of them to resist. Overcome by dopamine, they would initially behave like puppies needing to nuzzle. When their brains began to habituate to the dopamine cocktail, snuggling was no longer a fulfilling fix. Only sex would answer the call of their raging hormones.

That's where things got tricky. Claire was seductive but had no intention of offering consummation. She wanted to keep her suitors on the hook for as long as she could, short of providing that benefit.

Boys who had avoidant attachment styles would come on strong to Claire initially. When they began to feel the demands of her insecure attachment longings, they would begin to panic. They had no idea how to access their own deep, vulnerable emotions, let alone express them to another human being. The more they pulled away, the more Claire pursued and pleaded with them to stay. Without the offer of sex, their commitment was temporary. They just did not have the emotional resources to form a functional attachment bond at that point in their lives.

Claire had a couple of relationships with boys who had anxious attachment styles just as she did. To her surprise, they were as clingy and in need of assurance as she was. While she'd never felt she could get enough attention, with these boys she found herself feeling overwhelmed by the level of contact they required. They didn't seem to have minds of their own. They wanted to be with her all of the time and tended to let everyone around them know that they were dating long before Claire was ready to declare herself publicly.

Her serial disappointments in love only increased Claire's attachment insecurity. She struggled with deep feelings of shame and unworthiness. How else could she explain her failure to find someone who would help her navigate the perils of her emotions and circumstances?

Claire had difficulty waiting for the kind of person who could help her heal her attachment insecurity of the past. She had no vision of what such a creature would look and feel like. Instead, her chemistry and insecurity kept driving her to pursue new relationships that inevitably ended in traumatic, bitter breakups. All of this set the stage for meeting, conquering, and cohabiting with Ben.

## Committing to Commitment

It had indeed been love at first glance. Both Ben and Claire had felt it in every fiber of their beings. Their hearts had raced and their minds swirled with thoughts of their next moves. Childhood dreams and fantasies were within their grasp. Were the young lovers prepared for the most important commitment of their lives?

Most scientists, even evolutionary biologists, believe that the need for pair bonding is wired into human genetic code. Preparation for lifetime partnership begins when each person in the relationship expresses a desire for an exclusive lifelong love relationship. This can happen early or late in the dating cycle. Couples who are dopamine-driven may be obsessed with the euphoria of being in each other's presence. They might declare their intention to forge a lifelong love relationship early. If they have moral convictions that preclude sex before marriage, they might be motivated to marry as soon as possible. This could cause them to miss the slow steady benefits of dating for emotional attachment.

Attachment styles also motivate couples to declare their interest in a lifelong partnership. Men and women with anxious attachment styles may want to tie up the relationship quickly, out of insecurity. The person with an anxious attachment style will quickly cling to a lover. They have difficulty feeling secure in the relationship. They often overwhelm the person they are dating with their reaches of attention. They desperately want to feel secure and may influence their partner to commit too quickly.

This was certainly the case with Claire, who saw Ben as the stable, secure answer to all of the dating disappointments she had experienced in past relationships. Ben, with his avoidant attachment style, was initially dopamine-intoxicated by Claire's beauty and witty intelligence. He found himself saying, "yes, yes, yes" as she pursued him hard and fast. When he realized that she was offering him a genuine opportunity to close the deal for life, he began to get weak in the knees.

Ben wanted to fill his attachment loneliness, but when the relationship seemed to be closing in, he wanted to run from attachment. Every time he agreed to talk about marriage, he began to close down, become fearful, and pull back from Claire.

This was very confusing and hurtful to Claire, who would press in even harder. The pressure for commitment was frightening to Ben. Like a lot of avoiders, he had no awareness of his fear of emotional intimacy; he simply intellectualized it and offered a host of justifications for his distancing behavior.

Ben and Claire certainly had all of the facts to justify their union. They had the brains and the pedigrees to warrant sealing the deal. For Ben, Claire's stunning beauty was the big bonus that made him feel powerful and motivated to go all in.

Claire had been charmed and seduced by more than one handsome football star. She had her heart set on the secure future that a man like Ben could provide. Being a bright woman, she loved intellectually sparring with him. And, possibly of highest importance, she saw Ben as a man who could provide the financial security and the genetics for beautiful and talented children.

Rather than pay attention to their turbulent and at-times contradictory emotions, they decided to let their goals dictate their lifetime commitment to each other. Ben's career clock would be used as the motivator to seal the deal with a marriage ceremony. The decision to ignore emotional fears and push forward with success-driven goals would continue to set a pattern for them that would eventually lead to their marital crisis. They committed to each other, of course—in part driven by dopamine—but in a real way, they simply committed to commitment, not to real connection.

## Committing to Connection

Committing to connection rather than committing to commitment is a different way of defining the marital covenant. Committing to connection is committing to nurturing the emotions that will deepen and sustain the attachment bond. So many couples who make the decision to get married are placing their faith on their willpower rather than on their capacity to form and grow attachment bonds.

They think about marriage as being defined by a list of behaviors—things they will do only with each other and not with other people. These behaviors mainly involve sex. Most couples starting out in marriage agree that it is impossible to maintain trust without sexual exclusivity.

While it is true that sexual exclusivity is an essential foundation for trust, it alone does not build healthy attachment bonds. By committing to monogamy, as well as to the sharing of financial burdens, a couple constructs the walls of their house. But this is not the foundation.

The foundation of a strong, connected relationship involves a commitment to deepen the emotions that build strong attachment bonds. This has much more to do with *reassurance* than it does with *insurance*. It is impossible to ensure a relationship for lifetime love. No amount of commitment to love will ensure that a couple can withstand the ups and downs that life will throw at them.

No matter how much we believe that we have committed ourselves to another person for life, we are all destined to despair and divorce if we do not understand how to grow together in attachment. While close to fifty percent of married couples legally divorce, a large portion of the other remain miserably married, lacking in trust and deep attachment.

Engaging for attachment is about living life together in a way that deepens emotional bonds. It is a process of discovering what it feels like to have another person be there for you when you need him or her the most. It is a final test of emotional trust.

The power of the drive for more dopamine is part of what

fuels the deepening of the attachment relationship. By putting sex behind, rather than in front of the marital commitment, the couple can assess the security of the relationship without the drive for more and more dopamine.

The challenge ahead for Ben and Claire would be to understand the potential danger of dopamine-driven enticements in their fragile marriage, and to begin to rebuild their relationship in the context of attachment, not just sexual attraction. This would be the first step to move them from simple commitment to real connection.

part five
# adult
# attachment

## Love Left Behind
## and the Vital Science
## of Adult Attachment

STORY

# The Spiral
# of Disconnection

*A long marriage is two people trying to dance
a duet and two solos at the same time.*
—Anne Taylor Fleming

The weekend was nearing, and Claire had to finish her work on the Chicago travel story. With the kids at school and Ben at work, she'd finally have some quiet time. Claire grabbed her laptop and began to polish what she had begun three weeks earlier. Her deadline wasn't going to flex because of Ben's affair. *The hell with it . . . I'm not going to let my problems with Ben ruin my career.*

Claire attempted to close out all thoughts and emotions unrelated to her work. She had seen her husband do that hundreds of times. *Today's going to be about me. It's time for Claire, damn it.*

She had sorted through the myriad of pictures and was pleasantly reminded of her eye for composition and persistence in getting that perfect shot—the shot that would captivate and lure readers to whatever city or country she was documenting. Now, she would put the sparkle into her captions and prose to alleviate any question in her readers' minds that Chicago was the most incredible city on the planet.

Claire's job as a photojournalist had been important to her before and after she and Ben tied the knot. She couldn't imagine washing her talent and dreams down the drain just because of marriage. They both knew Ben would likely be the primary breadwinner, but Claire's contributions seemed as important. She loved the thought of leaving her imprint across the globe. So they had agreed: They would each have their own careers. While Ben was finishing his training and then setting up his medical practice, Claire would follow her dreams. She could scale down her work as necessary when the time came to raise kids.

From the start, Ben was busy with medicine, as anticipated, and Claire loved focusing on her career those first months. But she soon felt the loneliness creep in, slowly but surely, until it became overwhelming. The more her heart ached for something more in life, the more she threw herself into busyness. Her career flourished as a result of her dedication—work and friends filled some of the void—but there was still something missing. *God, I missed Ben. What happened to our taking the world by storm, together?*

And then along came Baby #1. Claire filled her lonely places with Jake.

Ben found a two-hour block in the middle of his day and decided that he had to get some exercise. He hopped on the gym's most obscured treadmill, careful to steer clear of scantily clad women flaunting their stuff. He didn't need some colleague to observe him talking to another woman. Besides, he wasn't proud of the extra few pounds he had picked up around his waistline. He was better off in his own quiet corner. Ben squeezed the excess roll around his middle and cursed under his breath. He had noticed Claire dropping pounds while he had certainly found them. *Stress . . . ain't it grand?* Ben's last treadmill exam had left the doctor concerned about his heart health. The warmth he often felt when his thoughts turned to Bridgette had apparently translated into higher blood pressure and serious acid reflux. This therapy process wasn't helping with any of that.

Ben increased his pace from a jog to a run, leaving puddles of sweat underfoot. He was alarmed by his racing heartbeat. He'd become less attentive to exercise these past months.

Knowing he might already have overdone it, Ben bypassed the weight machines, showered, and headed back uptown to the office. He programmed his alarm for his next patient, stretched out on the couch in his private office, still feeling his elevated heart rate, and quickly fell into a deep sleep.

If Ben had hoped to escape his circumstance by napping, it didn't work. In a dream, he found himself running, though not on a treadmill at the gym but out on the street, around and through the park where he sometimes jogged. There was someone running with him, but he couldn't make out who it was. It wasn't Claire. It wasn't Bridgette. His companion was hooded and never actually spoke.

Ben was doing all the talking. "There's something I still don't understand. This thing with Bridgette. I never intended it to happen. I mean, I wasn't looking for a relationship there. Even when Claire kind of shut down with me sexually, I wasn't looking for that from someone else. You see, that's just it—I wasn't looking for *something else*. I loved Claire."

Ben paused, then rephrased himself: "I *love* Claire."

Ben and his mystery companion jogged in sync and silence around the corner of the park. It was the park he was used to, but in the dream it was laid out differently and Ben couldn't figure out if he had just left his house or was at the end of his jog, running toward home.

"So, that's the thing," Ben continued. "I wasn't trying to have a relationship. I just plain wasn't even looking for someone else. Not looking at all. I love Claire. What the hell happened?"

The two runners came to a stoplight and jogged in place.

"Honestly," Ben said, "I know I was wrong to have let this happen. I was blind or naive or whatever—call me whatever name you want—but the fact is I walked myself straight into another relationship."

The light turned green and the two ran through the intersection together. Ben's companion said nothing, but Ben replied as if answering a question. "Really, I'm not sure I was ever in love with Bridgette. But letting go of her was more difficult than I thought it would be. I knew I had to end it. But, I have to say, even now it's tough when Claire is attacking me—and believe me, I get that, I understand that, she has every right to do that. But . . . here, on one side, Claire is attacking me and on the other side Bridgette is, well, being Bridgette . . . What would you do?"

Ben turned, only to find that his companion had disappeared. Looking around, he suddenly realized he was lost, alone, and had no idea where his home was.

The alarm sounded and Ben shot to his feet. He wiped sweat and the shame from his forehead.

"Of course we're going, Ben. This wedding has been on our calendar for months. John and Stacey would be crushed if we didn't make it."

Ben begrudgingly put on his black suit. He dreaded the evening. He ran through the likely guest list, preparing his phony smile and trivial conversation. Even on a good day, Ben didn't much like weddings—and this was not a good day—not a good *season*—for the two of them to attend a wedding. But he would go. And he would be on his best behavior.

Claire lost herself in their spacious suite. The eight pounds that stress had stolen from her allowed her to slide easily into her tight-fitted emerald sheath. Heels, classic pearls, and diamonds would perfectly complement the retro-style look she was going for.

Claire loved everything about weddings. Hers had been magical! Ben had let her and her mother have their way with most of the details, and even he had thought the day was epic. Claire examined her neatly made-up face in the mirror and fell silent in the memory. From the wedding to their European honeymoon, she could not have asked for more. She crinkled her forehead as she moved to the window and stared through the slatted blinds. The sun's rays lit her curls with golden fire.

A very *GQ*-looking Ben exited the walk-in closet.

"Remember our wedding, Ben? When did we lose that magic? Was it all a big lie? Has our entire marriage been a farce?"

Ben's tone was rough now. "Claire, aren't you being a bit dramatic? A *farce*? We had a plan and we're living it. Tell me, what have you wanted that you don't have? We've got two beautiful kids, a gorgeous home in one of Chicago's finest suburbs . . . Did all that come from a lie, Claire? Your friends look at our life and see plenty of magic. Why can't you? If you want to know the truth, I'd love to trade my twelve-hour days at the office for some of your *lost magic*."

Claire's big eyes welled with tears as she felt the weight of Ben's words. His raised voice brought her insecurity into focus. She was flooded with fear of losing him. Claire was accustomed to passivity from Ben. Normally, she couldn't shake him into an argument; he would just sit and flip the pages of the newspaper while her taunts escalated. This was something new from Ben, and it scared her.

The room was dead with silence. Breaking the quiet with her soft, fearful, and child-like voice, Claire whispered, "I'm afraid, Ben. I'm sorry. I can't imagine being alone."

"Claire, I'm not planning to leave you. I told you that. I've ended things with Bridgette. Why can't you trust me?" Ben recognized the distant look on her face, and he knew exactly what his wife was remembering. *Please don't go there again, Claire.*

Claire slid into the nine-year-old memory. Deeply etched on her heart was the experience of being alone during the birth of their son. Any trigger of her fear of abandonment took her back to that moment, and the question, *could Ben really be there for her* *when she needed him?* Would he bail on her? He had known she was expected to deliver early. It was just two weeks short of her actual due date, and he had left her to go to a medical conference. She had never been able to forgive him for that.

Ben insisted that the conference was important, and, though Claire expressed her fear about him leaving, he chose to go anyway. It was only four hours away, he said, but that proved beside the point when his cell phone went dead. He didn't get the call until it was too late. Claire delivered their first child with her mother at her side and Ben 300 miles north. Claire's parents held their baby boy before Ben did. She had felt utterly deserted at the biggest moment of her life. Now, her fear of abandonment waited in the wings for any opportunity to rear its horribly ugly head.

Claire had begun to lose trust in her husband nine years earlier. She still wondered if she could count on him to be there for her.

Not another word passed between them until they reached the church. Claire was a wreck and wondered if she was even capable of getting through the ceremony. Her friends couldn't know just how miserable she was and what a mess their marriage was in. Only her sister knew of Ben's affair. That's how it would stay.

Claire sat through the exchange of vows silently repeating every word. She thought about how easy it was to say those words, make those promises, without knowing what a life together really required. She thought about how easy it was for a few words to end a marriage and leave one alone forever.

Ben's mind wandered through most of the service. His earlier fight with Claire had rattled him, and now he used his time in the pew to regroup.

He traced his thoughts back to his safe place. Bridgette. He replayed their meeting of a few nights back when he had said goodbye to her forever. Yes, he had regrets about that. About leaving the comfort of Bridgette behind. But there was no question in his mind that he would stay married to Claire. He just wanted—needed—it to be different between them.

Ben was totally lost in thought when Claire elbowed him. "I pronounce you husband and wife" echoed in the sanctuary as he returned to the here and now. *Husband and wife. Do they have any idea what they're getting into?*

Ben and Claire had been to several weddings in the previous year. So many of their young physician friends were tying the knot. This reception was over-the-top, no cost spared. Clearly the young bride's parents were well off.

Claire got caught in a conversation as they moved through the reception line, and Ben moved on without her. When Claire looked up again, she realized she'd lost him. Where was he? There. She saw him at the wine bar.

Claire made her way across the ballroom floor, drawing admiring stares as she moved. If only she felt as amazing as she looked. Though she was mad at Ben, she still needed him close by.

Claire came up behind Ben, tuning in to the conversation he

was having, something about Wednesday night and "hush-hush." The distinguished gentleman, fifty-something, was a familiar face to Claire. Dr. Smith. She knew his wife, Sandra.

The color drained from Ben's face as he realized Claire was now beside him.

"Hello, Claire." The doctor's large hand kindly met hers. "Unfortunately Sandra couldn't make it tonight. A touch of the flu, I'm afraid."

"So sorry to hear that," Claire replied. "I'll need to reconnect with her when she's better. We've been so busy of late and haven't been able to get out much—"

Ben interrupted, "As I was saying, I was intrigued by what you said at the conference, and we're going to have to talk about that when we have more time. Unfortunately, we need to grab the groom for a few words before the dancing starts." Ben almost seemed to be shooing Smith off. A moment later, he was steering Claire toward the wine bar.

"Well, that seemed rude, Ben. You sure got rid of him quickly."

"He and I were done with our conversation. And, if he starts talking, there's no stopping him. Let's grab some wine and get away from this crowd."

Claire clutched her husband's arm as he whisked her toward the outdoor patio. "Geez, slow down. What's up with you?"

Ben wanted to run from Claire, from this place. He had not anticipated seeing Smith on Wednesday night, while meeting with Bridgette, and he was horrified to see him again tonight. He certainly didn't want to have to explain everything to Claire.

"Ben, I heard him say something about Wednesday night staying between the two of you. What was that about? You had that business meeting Wednesday night, right? Why would that need to be hush-hush?" Her loud voice drew attention.

Ben grabbed Claire's arm, somewhat roughly, and pulled her away from the crowd.

"Stop it, Ben. Stop pulling on me. What are you doing?" Claire's eyes filled with tears. "What are you hiding? Does Smith know about your girlfriend? What the hell's going on with you?"

"Lower you voice, Claire. People are staring. Do we really need to do this here?" Ben looked at the ground and fidgeted, feeling humiliated. "My Wednesday meeting was canceled and I met Bridgette instead. I wanted to end things between us."

"You what? You saw her and didn't tell me? You keep telling me to trust you, and now this! Another lie. Another secret meeting. I can't believe you, Ben. How do you expect me to trust you when you keep lying?"

Claire didn't give Ben a chance to explain. She was on a roll and didn't care who heard her. Ben was a lying cheater. "So, what about Dr. Smith? He saw you, I suppose? Oh my god, he saw you. That's awesome, Ben. A department chair sees you with another woman. I guess you don't even care about your reputation. *Our* reputation."

Uncomfortable bystanders began to disperse, giving Ben and Claire their space.

Ben was frozen in fear as Claire pierced into the truth of his deception. No one cared more about Ben's reputation than Ben did. He was the rising star among his peers, always doing the right thing even when it was difficult. Now, he'd gotten caught in his own web of lies. He couldn't believe it.

"Let's go," Claire said. "We're not going to stand here and ruin John and Stacey's special day. You've already ruined it for me. Let's just leave and hope no one notices. Or, you could make up another lie, Ben. That seems to come pretty naturally for you these days."

Ben and Claire stormed off to their car without speaking.

When a friend called out from a distance, Ben turned and, with a slight wave, said he had been called away on an emergency. Claire was steaming, too embarrassed to look back.

She was glad to get into the house after an excruciating forty-minute drive. She pulled the pins from her upswept hair and felt the weight of her curls fall to her tight shoulders. She slipped out of her heels and the gorgeous dress that had barely had time to wrinkle.

Ben wished he could rewind the clock. He didn't have the energy to engage in a heated battle tonight, or even to be a quiet recipient of Claire's out-of-control emotions. He had learned from his father that it was best to quietly absorb a degree of his wife's panic, and then slip away into a safe corner where he could process his thoughts internally. He quietly disappeared into his study, hoping to be left alone.

He was surprised by Claire's calm entrance.

"I know it would be much easier, Ben, to put this night behind us and move on. I can't do that. We need to talk."

Ben knew he wouldn't get off easy. This would be a long night.

"You know, Ben, even if there weren't another woman in the picture, our marriage would still be in trouble. I think we both know that. When did we become such strangers? We don't talk. We rarely make love or even touch anymore. That really scares me. This is a bigger problem than Bridgette, isn't it?"

Ben sat quietly and processed her words, then cautiously formed his reply. "Claire, the reality is, we began drifting apart when Jake was born. And then when Leslie came along, it just got worse. This has been going on for years. I know you think raising the kids is your primary purpose in life. And right behind them, it's your sister and friends. And your work—it's truly important—your art, what it is and can be in the world. And there's my work, too. I understand that. But—" Then, carefully crafting his next words, Ben said softly, "I feel like I get scraps."

Ben had seen all her friends prioritizing just like Claire. And their husbands were all feeling like he was. They just assumed this was what you did when the babies came. They had no idea when all that would change, so they resigned themselves to a lonely coexistence.

He continued, "I think it's great that you have so many friends. And I'm really proud of the way you've become so involved with school and community events. People don't know how lucky they are to have you chairing all the committees you do, leading in so many ways. And, again, your photography—I wish, honestly, I had the creative talent you have. You've been a fantastic mother. I never worry about our kids. They are so fortunate to have you for a mom . . ."

"Ben, you're laying it on kind of thick, aren't you? I see what you're doing."

Ben didn't allow her to break his stride. "No, Claire, no, you aren't going to write my words for me. This is what I feel and honestly believe. Claire, I think you are fantastic. But here's the thing: A lot of people get the best of you. But me, well, I sometimes feel like I'm just a guy, another person in line. I just don't feel like I'm a priority to you."

Claire remained silent for a moment. "Well, thanks. I guess there's some sort of compliment in there. But I sure don't feel like a fantastic anything right now." Claire choked back a sob. "If I'm so awesome, why did you go after someone else? I know we don't have sex like we used to. We're both pretty exhausted by the end of the day. I used to really want you, Ben. I loved our long and close hugs. Remember how we used to take long walks holding hands and planning our future?"

"Hey, I remember all that, too. I gave up on approaching you for sex and closeness and walks long ago. You didn't seem to have the time or interest in being with me. I tried to suck it up, and I did. I understand that couples go through seasons in life; I figured we were going through ours. But I had no idea how much I was starving for your affection. I figured we'd get back to being a couple when the kids were older. But now, I'm not sure that's how it's supposed to work."

"Yeah, obviously you couldn't wait. You know, Ben, even if you didn't have sex with Bridgette, you shared your heart with her. That very heart that you supposedly gave to me ten years ago. Can you even imagine what it would feel like if I did that to you?"

"Actually, yes. I have felt it for the last five years, when everything and everyone in your life seemed more important than me. Yes, Claire. I've been studying and working my butt off trying to get licensed and get the practice up and running. For us. For our family. And you pretty much left me alone." A softness came over him. "So, yes, I do know what it feels like."

Claire had no idea her husband had even cared that she had become so busy with other things. Yet she wasn't about to let him completely turn the tables on her. "We agreed on all this. Except the affair part, that is. I take care of the kids. You get the practice running well, bring some associates on board, and then focus on us, me and the kids. That was our agreement. Let's be real here. Do you really think that will ever happen? I mean the 'more time for us' part?"

"I think I'm saying that very thing. Only I came to think that, to you, 'time for us' didn't actually include me."

Claire fell silent.

Ben knew when it was time to withdraw from the battle. "I don't know, Claire," he said. "I don't have the answers, that's for sure."

"I don't either," Claire replied softly.

Ben was caught off guard by what came out of his mouth next—and more so by the fact that he truly meant it. "I know this, though. I have no intention of leaving you and the kids. I'm not sure how we'll fix all this, but I am going to do my part." He paused, then added, "I want to come home, Claire."

And that was about all the emotion Ben could eke out. Exhausted, he pleaded for an adjournment, at least for the night.

Claire felt some calm come over her. "Okay, Ben. And . . . thank you."

Having been given leave, Ben needed to swerve out of the emotional vortex. He sighed a deep sigh. After a few moments, he reached for the remote, switched on the TV, and began flipping through the channels. "You want to watch something?"

Numb and yet strangely relieved, Claire curled her long legs underneath her and pulled an afghan over her shoulders. "Sure, Ben. Whatever looks good." The two sat in silence for another hour before Claire snuck off for a warm shower.

Later, she fell between her soft sheets and found peace in the rhythmic flickering of the gazebo lights out back.

THERAPY

# From Withdrawal to Engagement

*When you really listen to another person from their point of
view, and reflect back to them that understanding, it's like
giving them emotional oxygen.*
–Stephen Covey

Ten minutes before Ben and Claire arrived, I made a quick
visit to the bathroom, refilled my glass with cold water, and
pulled up their progress notes from the last session. I needed to
have the context of where we left off to keep the therapy moving.

Last week, we processed the big picture of how new love relationships create a kind of temporary insanity. We also began to
bump up against the reality that Ben and Claire began to lose each
other shortly after they said, "I do." In this session, I would work
on trying to get Ben in touch with his deep, complex emotions of
hurt and fear of losing Claire. If he doesn't speak to Claire through
his emotions, there is no way that she will trust him again, no
matter what he says.

**Therapist:** What's been happening with the two of you since we met last?

**Ben:** I thought we were making progress after last week's session. Things were pretty calm during the week.

**Claire:** We were back into our old routine of Ben working late and my being helicopter mom. We really didn't talk much. I was still feeling horrible on the inside, but I thought I would save it for therapy. Then the weekend came and things went downhill fast.

They went on to tell me about the wedding. It was interesting to me that Claire spoke about the memories the event stirred up in her of their own wedding. At one point, she said, "It reminded me how much I loved our wedding and also how much I love Ben." She spoke about loving him in the present tense. Other times, Claire talked about how she had *once* loved Ben—in the past tense. I sensed this reflected her current tension regarding their marriage—both statements were true.

Ben, meanwhile, had dreaded the wedding, in part because he was afraid of running into his doctor friend there and knew that he'd need to manage a potentially messy scene. He'd worried about how he could keep Claire and Dr. Smith apart. Of course, all of that blew up in their faces.

And yet, despite the scene that took place at the wedding, I sensed there was something different between them. Claire was a little less likely to lash out accusingly at Ben, and Ben was not defending himself as much anymore. I learned of a deeper conversation the two had had later the night of the wedding.

**Therapist:** So, you spoke about your fears of losing each other. Ben, what are you feeling when you hear how deeply Claire is grieving about losing you?

**Ben:** I have tried to tell her that I am not going anywhere.

**Therapist:** I know. But what are you *feeling* about that?

**Ben:** I feel terrible. And afraid. I can't believe that this is happening to us either. I can't believe that we let ourselves grow so far apart and that I did this stupid thing! I never intended to betray Claire or destroy our relationship.

**Therapist:** So, you are afraid and sorry about what has happened to your relationship. And how you have betrayed Claire?

**Ben:** Yes, I am.

**Therapist:** Ben, do you think you could tell Claire that?

**Ben:** Yes. I think I have.

**Therapist:** I mean right now.

**Ben:** Now? Oh. Okay . . . so, yes, I admit I have betrayed Claire, and—

**Therapist:** Ben, I'm asking you to tell Claire, not me. And I'm asking you to express how you *feel* about what you've done.

**Ben:** *(Looks at me, blinks, then nods and slowly turns toward Claire. Starts to speak, then stops. Looks back at me.)* This is hard.

**Therapist:** Yes. It is. This is the point of change for you. Expressing your emotions—it's not a weakness.

**Ben:** *(Faces Claire)* I, uh . . . Well, the worst moment in my entire life happened when you walked in that day. It was my phone, the messages, that scene, when it came out. In that moment, I knew

142

you knew—about Bridgette. At first I was just afraid—for myself, how this would change my life—and then I looked into your eyes. There, in a flash of a second, I saw your hurt. It was a kind of agony inside you. It felt to me like I had stabbed you with something—physically wounded you. I realized then how utterly cruel I was by doing what I'd done. It broke me apart inside to feel even a little of your pain and know how I had caused it. I felt so terrible. So guilty. So sad about what I had done to you. (*Ben stops. Tears are now streaming down his face. He appears shaken and fragile. He has Claire's full attention.*)

**Therapist:** Take your time . . .

**Ben:** (*Nods. Takes a deep breath*) Well, I felt an urgency to undo this terrible thing. Maybe I just couldn't believe I'd done this to you and I wanted to minimize it, like you do when one of the kids scrapes a knee—

**Claire:** (*Tears in her eyes*) This wasn't a scraped knee, Ben.

**Ben:** No, it wasn't. And, believe me, I knew that so very well from that moment, looking into your eyes. But in my urgency to undo the hurt I had caused you, I was desperate to make it smaller, walk it back, make it fade away. That was more about me, I know that now. I felt so ashamed about how I'd hurt you, I wanted just to sweep it under. (*Ben pauses. He is crying. Tears are welling up in Claire's eyes, too. There is silence.*)

**Therapist:** Claire, you hear these words about how remorseful Ben is. Do you believe these feelings in him?

**Claire:** (*Slowly nodding*) I mean, I feel he's lied to me so often, I don't know what to believe. But I hear this, and yes—

**Therapist:** Claire, tell your feelings to Ben, not me.

**Claire:** (*Turns toward Ben*) Yes, Ben . . . I sometimes don't know what to believe . . . but, I have to say, I have never seen you reveal this much emotion to me. I see how sorry you are for hurting me. I just don't understand how you could have done this to us. I completely trusted you.

**Ben:** I understand how much I have hurt you and damaged your trust in me—I mean, more than that—it's like I *feel* that hurt in you and that loss of trust. I want you to know that I want to fight for our marriage. This other relationship opened up emotions in me that I didn't know were there. I want us to find our way back to the connection that we had in the beginning.

**Therapist:** Claire, could you tell Ben what you were feeling when he said that he wanted you to trust him again and reconnect with you?

**Claire:** (*To Ben*) I just feel so hurt and confused right now. I want that, too. It's not just the affair. There were so many times I needed you in the past when your absence deeply hurt me. I just gave up expecting that you would be there for me. I never stopped loving you. I just thought that this was the way life would be, with you practicing medicine and me raising the kids. But you being unfaithful was not on my radar.

**Ben:** It wasn't on my radar either. I never intended for the relationship to go where it did. It started out as just a working relationship and then migrated into a friendship. And then something deeper. I began to rely on Bridgette as a confidant, and it just spiraled from there. I never intended to hurt you, but looking back, I don't know how I could have imagined it wouldn't.

**Claire:** I made things work, but I was dying on the inside. I was so lonely. Someone had to be there for the kids. It felt like I just had to survive the growing distance between us. But I was committed to make it work. I trusted you to be committed, too.

**Therapist:** Claire, it hurts you deeply that Ben violated your covenant when you were so committed to be faithful, even as it felt like you were dying inside.

**Claire:** That's right.

**Therapist:** So you thought your commitment to each other would keep the relationship secure even if the connection was breaking down.

**Claire:** I thought the connection would restore itself when we were less busy.

What Claire said right then is, I believe, the key to so many marriage issues. Couples without regular, daily, true connection count on their commitment—their marriage vows—to save their marriage. They think that in another time, a better time, a less busy time, their connection will magically come back. It doesn't. Until something traumatic happens and everything is on the line.

I spoke with Ben and Claire about some of my observations. Each of them had different kinds of insecurities they'd brought into the marriage from their relationship histories. Claire had a pattern of reaching for the relationship when she was insecure; yet this wasn't really about the real Ben—it was about satisfying her insecurity by filling up on status and performance—what felt to Ben to be sheer pretense.

Ben had a pattern of withdrawing from the relationship when he was insecure; that insecurity had a lot to do with emotions he didn't feel comfortable processing. But all of us have emotions and an inner need to express them. Bridgette showed up and became what seemed like a safe, arm's-length outlet for Ben to share the feelings he couldn't express otherwise.

Both Ben and Claire came into the marriage with adult attachment insecurities. These are deep and foundational, and over time they can take over one's life, as well as the life of a marriage. Unless couples spend time early on working through their insecurities, these patterns will rise up later in the marriage, as they have with Ben and Claire. Often, the problem is that marriages are usually based on the early, dopamine-driven chemical rush of new love and never progress to a deeper openness about insecurities, needs, and true feelings.

The session continued, but the biggest breakthrough had already happened. Ben had turned a corner, and it wasn't just in the hour we had together that day. Something had been percolating in him since the previous session. I was pleased to see Ben step forward and own what his betrayal had done to Claire. Betrayal can never be brushed off or excused, even if there is intimacy deprivation. At the same time, it is important for both people in the relationship to see the big picture of what led to this crisis and what they need to do to repair it.

While it was clear to me that Claire was not yet ready to forgive Ben and let him in, the ground for that had been prepared. It was Ben who had been withdrawing from her for years, and he needed to step forward first. Emotionally opening up would be easier for Claire once she knew she was safe.

But Ben would need to be there to catch her heart when she let it go.

SCIENCE

# The Big Picture of
# Adult Attachment

*Feeling close and complete with someone else [is] the emo-
tional equivalent of finding a home . . .*

—Amir Levine, *Attached: The New Science of Adult Attachment and
How It Can Help You Find—and Keep—Love*

The problem is, we can't fool human nature.

We are biologically wired to need connection that lasts well
beyond the days of dopamine-driven feelings. Feeling secure
depends on our knowing that there is at least one significant other
who we can count on when the going gets tough. We survive and
thrive by sharing our needs for emotional love and support with
another person. When we do not have another person with whom
we can share our deepest feelings, we begin to disintegrate, emotionally and physically.

There is no place lonelier than a committed relationship where
the dopamine has died and the partners have not learned how
to create a secure emotional connection. Ben and Claire had not
found a bonding connection. As their lives became more parallel,
they each, in different ways, found themselves fearfully lonely.

## Adult Attachment Breakthrough

In 1987, researchers Cindy Hazan and Philip Shaver from the University of Denver performed a study to build upon the discoveries of Bowlby and Ainsworth. They set out to test whether adults express the same kind of secure and insecure attachment styles that children do. They designed a clever attachment-style quiz that they published in the *Rocky Mountain News*. To their astonishment, they found that the percentages of adults who were secure (56 percent), avoidant (25 percent), and anxious/ambivalent (19 percent), mirrored almost exactly what Ainsworth had discovered about infants.[14] While this study was based on survey methods and was considered non-scientific, it broke open a wave of adult attachment research that exists to this day.

In the mid 1980s it was a psychologist named Sue Johnson, attending university in Canada, who, with the help of her professor Les Greenberg, made the connection between the threat of losing attachment bonds and marital distress.

After watching thousands of hours of video of couples in conflict, it occurred to Sue that it was the *risk to attachment bonds* that was at the root of the emotions. When adults' attachment bonds are threatened, they move into primitive fight-or-flight emotions, just as infants do when left alone. This discovery led her to pioneer a new form of psychotherapy for couples that focuses on repairing these attachment-based emotions. This new approach, Emotionally Focused Therapy (EFT) was the hope for saving Ben and Claire's marriage.

## The Importance of Emotional Memory

The focus on emotions, rather than on thoughts, paved the way for researchers to crack the code of what makes love go well or badly in adult love relationships. Again, the parallel between infant and adult love could not be more apparent.

148

Our memories of our most important life events are embedded in our emotions. Recalling these memories often ignites feelings of joy, sadness, or even terror years later. Every relationship has an emotional life map that provides markers for how the couple has felt about life and each other throughout the course of the relationship. How we relate to each other in the present has a lot to do with these emotional markers. They inform us ahead of time that we can expect to feel a certain way when a certain thing happens.

The emotional memory maps created by past relationships are often imposed on a marriage. Our collective experience with connection makes us resistant, welcoming, or receptive to the emotions of our spouse. Emotions are at the foundation of the attachment styles that Ainsworth discovered in her infant observation studies, and they are the glue that forms the attachment bonds that keep us connected or in conflict.

In new relationships, we are flooded with passionate emotions that draw us to another person. As our relationships mature, we experience less new-love passion, and may easily underestimate how emotions continue to be the key to how we organize our interactions with the person we love.

Early in a relationship, we become very aware of what triggers an emotional response in our partner, as well as what our partner can do to trigger an emotional response in us. We are constantly making adjustments and accommodations for the incoming emotional missiles launched at us, sometimes at the most unexpected times. Our defenses remain on high alert, ready to protect us in the event that we spot an incoming emotion that threatens to flood us with emotional pain.

The denial of the importance of emotion decreases our ability to weather the emotional storms that come up in every close relationship. When we disconnect from our emotional warning-

and-response system, we disarm our most important form of navigation to care for our partner and ourselves. Thinking and rational strategies are simply no match for emotional intelligence when it comes to making relationships work. Even bright and talented Ben could not strategize his way through the marital conflict he found himself in.

Ben had spent most of his childhood and adult life believing that emotions would get in his way. Like his father and many others, he thought he had no need for the troublesome annoyance of emotion. As we worked through the steps of EFT, he began to learn that he did have emotion, although he had carefully and very successfully stuffed it so far away that he was taken aback when it emerged.

Claire's emotions were erratic. She felt justified for what Ben labeled as being "out-of-control." She soaked many tissues and shirtsleeves with deeply felt tears in weekly therapy sessions.

Because Ben was blocked from his own emotions, he could not identify with Claire's. He had no intuitive understanding of her needs. Because his emotional response system was offline, he could not navigate relationship conflict. This is always a problem for therapists when helping couples to grow in intimacy.

Solving conflict requires that each person read what the emotional hurt is all about. The surface or secondary emotions do not convey the depth of the emotional pain. A secondary emotion of anger is often a cover for the deep feelings of abandonment that occur when a partner feels ignored or betrayed. Loving another person requires us to be non-defensive and take the time to help our partner express the pain beneath the angry protest.

If we are easily hurt and fire anger back when fired upon, we find ourselves caught in negative cycles of emotional interaction that make it impossible to resolve conflict. There is no end to how we can set up "rational" explanations for why we do the things we do. Soon we sound like two lawyers arguing their positions rather than two lovers who care about each other's emotional pain.

This is what happened to Ben and Claire.

## Attachment and Health

Neuroscientists now know that emotions have everything to do with mental and physical health. The brain and body thrive in the presence of positive emotion and become sick when emotions turn negative. Relationships respond in the same way. But it is relationships that are at the heart of creating the conditions for a happy or sad emotional state of being. While each of us can improve the way we regulate emotions, through the practice of meditation or what Martin Seligman calls "learned optimism," none of us exist healthy in isolation.

We are wired for connection, and it is connection that forms the foundation of a healthy rewarding emotional life.

The absence of health is disease (*dis-ease*). When we have a disease, we no longer live in the *ease* of feeling and functioning without struggle. Love relationship problems contribute more to disease than most of us comprehend.

Science is now looking at the links between health and attachment. What is being discovered is astounding.

The emotion of fear signals danger ahead. It triggers powerful fight-or-flight neurochemistry that causes us to take immediate action. When the perception of danger triggers a fear response, the part of our brain called the *amygdala* sends out signals that trigger the release of cortisol and epinephrine. These powerful stress hormones speed up heart rate, raise blood pressure and produce feelings of anxiety, which trigger fight-or-flight responses. When we are easily triggered by fear, we struggle with risk-taking and making connections with other people. This can eventually lead to chronic anxiety and depression.

Researcher Dr. James Coan tested the relationship of fear to attachment bonds. He put women in fMRI machines and told them that when the red light was on they would receive an electric shock.[15] The results of the study were fascinating. Women who held the hand of their husbands experienced less fear activation in the brain than women who were on their own. The women who were most attached to their husbands (emotionally as well as physically) had barely noticeable fear responses to the shocks.

Are you beginning to see the importance of attachment? Dr. Coan concluded that "at the deepest level, we hold hands to send each other's brains a signal, something like, 'I am here with you.' Over time, that signal becomes stronger until it would appear that the simple act of holding hands unites two people as one with an, 'I am you,' to the point that even the brain believes this!"

This secure attachment bond that decreases fear has other remarkable health benefits. Jim Coyne at the University of Pennsylvania found that, after heart failure, marital connection was as good a predictor of recovery as the symptoms of the heart attack or the degree of impairment.[16] Healthy attachment has been found to lower hypertension. Unhealthy attachment has been found to elevate hypertension when one is in the proximity of the person he or she is attached to.[17]

Lack of attachment produces deep feelings of loneliness, and loneliness has been found to double our chance of stroke or heart attack.[18] After reviewing the research on loneliness, James House at the University of Michigan concluded that emotional isolation is more dangerous than cigarette smoking.

The stress produced by the threat of losing an attachment bond has significant affects on our capacity to heal. Janice Kiecolt Glacer conducted a study with newlyweds,[19] creating a condition that caused them to fight in the laboratory. She found that the fighting produced higher stress hormones in the blood. The blisters that were created by a suction device on the female newlyweds' hands healed more slowly for those in the most hostile fights.

When we are securely attached, we have a greater capacity to seek support and show empathy and love. Jeff Simpson (University of Minnesota) conducted an experiment with eighty-three dating couples. The female partners were warned that they would be made anxious in the experiment. The attached females were able to state their fears and seek support. The unattached women avoided closeness and were more likely to withdraw. The attached men showed more support through touching, smiling, and comfort. The unattached men were less sympathetic toward their partners, touched them less, and downplayed their distress.[20]

Our view of ourselves is profoundly affected by how attached we are. There is a popular notion that we need to love ourselves before we can love others. Growing research suggests that we cannot love ourselves *unless others love us.* Mario Mikulincer at Bar Ilan University in Israel found that securely attached adults were less self-critical than those with insecure attachments.[21] They were more open to new information, better at problem solving, and had more positive goals. He also found that they were better able to revise their assessments of others and had less anger and malicious intent toward their partners.

Brook Feeney at Carnegie Mellon's Relationship Lab also validated the link between connection in relationships and personal achievement.[22] She found that when partners support each other's goals, each person had greater confidence, self-esteem, and an elevated mood. When partners did not support each other's goals, they were less confident about achieving those goals and downgraded the importance of them.

What all of this research boils down to is that *attachment is the great organizer of our internal biological processing, our emotional experience and our view of self and others.* Attachment health may be the single most important foundation for physical, emotional, and relational health, and our capacity to live up to our peak potential. Without secure attached relationships, we limp through life struggling from the inside out. Moments of brilliance are unsustainable.

We do not have to look far to see great examples of crashing and burning after achieving great success. The movie industry makes the heartbreak of serial relationships sexy. Wall Street makes narcissism and the incapacity to connect a prerequisite of iconic leadership. The medical profession worships physicians who run roughshod over the emotions of the people they work with. (The successful TV series *House* offered a perfect example of this.)

There is much ignorance surrounding the importance of emotions and attachment, and it must be addressed if we are to improve our health as a global community. The science of the past, which tended to elevate intellect above emotion and attachment, has caused great damage to the age-old institutions of marital fidelity, mother love, father love, and community loyalty.

Thanks to ongoing scientific research, a new era has dawned in our understanding of the crucial importance of emotions in the forming of attachment bonds. While much of popular culture still lives in emotional-attachment darkness, the new relational neuroscience is shining a bright light on the truth of our most fundamental needs and motivations. *We are created for connection, and this connection is the foundation for our wholeness and our capacity to live up to our full potential.*

## The Job and Parent Trap:
## Setting Family and Career Priorities

During the early years of marriage, nearly all couples are consumed with the twin desires of making career advances and starting a family. Both our biology and the realities of life pull on us to do these things better and faster. While many couples wait a number of years before having children, it is often for the sake of getting ahead with career. For most of their relationship, Ben and Claire were consumed with career and children.

Research has shown that marital satisfaction decreases when children are introduced into the relationship. It is only after they grow up and leave home that marital satisfaction returns to pre-child-rearing levels. If a couple can stay together through child rearing, they often find even greater marital satisfaction than they'd enjoyed during their early, pre-child relationship.

When couples get married, dopamine levels begin to drop, and with that, the lusty love that brought them together. Seeing your spouse naked is still fun but does not have the same impact that it did before marriage. Sex being slightly out of reach is what activates the dopamine system. When couples say I do, the brain begins to shut down the powerful dopamine system designed to create magnetic, new-love attraction.

When energy levels are drained by the demands of work and children, it may become difficult to find the time to stir passion into action. The saying "use it or lose it" is true when it comes to sex. Couples who stop having sex regularly often experience problems with sexual performance, even in their thirties and forties. The decrease in desire and misfires in bed can result in a self-consciousness that erodes the sexual confidence of earlier years.

After Ben and Claire's first child was born, Ben stood back, as many new fathers do. He had no clue as to how to meet Claire's emotional needs at that point. When he didn't meet her needs for attachment, Claire began to let her baby fulfill those needs, and baby became her primary attachment. This left Claire empty of the adult love fulfillment that only Ben could give her.

Placing kids and career before intimacy in marriage results

in deep feelings of loneliness that couples often have difficulty talking about. The busyness of the early years of marriage doesn't help, as it often results in "talking time" being placed on the back burner. Soon, they have gotten out of the habit of talking about how they feel about each other and what they need.

Then the intimate emotions that make couples feel safe, loved, and secure are not given primary importance. The empty loneliness that results is filled with the multiple activities of work and household. A kind of "hardening of the arteries" sets into the hearts of married couples that don't take the time to form intimate connections. They have difficulty being softhearted with each other, even when one partner is in need. Wives sometimes turn to other women for support, rather than to their husbands; likewise, men sometimes turn to other men—which can be like the blind leading the blind. They may also deal with their unmet sexual needs by dabbling in pornography. This can escalate into a full-blown sexual addiction, in which the dopamine system fires up at the first glance of a new naked body or at the first words of sexual play.

It is common for men and women to turn to alcohol to take the edge off of the stress and relationship emptiness they feel. It seems innocent enough to have a glass or two or even three after work. The problem is, when couples rely on alcohol to numb their pain rather than turning to each other for emotional support, they miss out on the opportunity to express and feel the emotions that will draw them together in an authentic way.

Men and women often fall prey to the sympathetic ears of others who may also be struggling with intimacy issues. The dopamine high of this new relationship can fool struggling marital partners into believing that they made the wrong choice of a spouse. When an established marriage is compared with the emotional high of an affair, there is no contest as to which one is going to feel more exciting.

Claire found some safety in social groups and church activities. Ben found safety in work-related conferences. It felt safer to both of them to discuss their increasing marital disconnection with less significant others than with each other. Claire's go-to listening ear was her sister, and soon her relationship with Steph gained primacy over that with Ben. Though Ben and Claire's outside relationships felt like safe places to share, they should have been off-limits for marital matters between husband and wife. Too often, outside relationships are a forum for pouring out the matters of our hearts to the wrong people.

Relationships outside of marriage can be used to provide the sense of connection people are missing in their marriages. In the right balance, they are a healthy and good addition to the marriage relationship. However, they are not a substitution for true marital intimacy.

In looking for fulfillment of their attachment needs, Ben and Claire failed to turn to each other and work together. Instead, they each turned elsewhere to fill up their lives.

Ben and Claire were finally starting to turn toward each other in therapy. It would be interesting to see if they could rebuild their connection.

part six

# committed
to
# connection

Empty and Alone:
Hope Through Healing

15

## STORY

# Courage to Connect

*Romantic love is not the least bit illogical or random.
It is the continuation of an ordered and
wise recipe for survival.*
—Dr. Sue Johnson

Between patients, Ben stared into space, reflecting and churning on the last therapy session. *I must have looked like a fool, crying in front of the therapist and Claire,* he thought. And yet he knew he didn't need to think that way. There was something in all he was being told that he knew was right. The mirror being held up reflected something true about him: He was paralyzed emotionally. He couldn't deny it.

In the house with Claire, things were still awkward and tight, yet there were occasional improvements. What he had said in therapy about "wanting to come home" was from his heart. It seemed Claire had heard that and had made some effort toward making the house once again Ben's home, too. If it wasn't normalcy, it was marginally better. Still, too often Ben felt the gaze of distrust from Claire.

It seemed like forever since he had talked with Bridgette. Thoughts of her . . . well, they continued to drift in and out, but they were fewer and farther between. He was now careful to dismiss such thoughts before they took hold, and maybe as a result—or just because of the passage of time—Bridgette was becoming a distant object in the rearview mirror. Clearly, not for Claire, though; not yet anyway.

Ben was startled by the phone's ring, and for just a moment, he wondered. . . His quick glance revealed a caller ID that was neither Bridgette's nor Claire's.

"Ben, it's Dr. Smith. Do you have a minute?"

Ben froze, his heart sinking. Dr. Smith had been so respectful of Ben's privacy, careful not to expose his secret meeting with Bridgette. Now what? Ben sunk in his chair and braced for the confrontation.

"Hi, Ben. Hope you and Claire are well."

Silence, as Ben found he couldn't get even a couple of words out.

"Hey," Smith plowed on, "I wanted to throw something out there. As you've probably heard, I'm planning for my retirement. It's still a year off, but that's going to be here sooner than I can imagine."

This was not the conversation Ben expected.

"Ben, I want to recommend you for the Department Chair position when I leave."

Ben couldn't believe his ears. Apparently, his personal affairs were of no concern to Smith after all. With a deep sigh of relief, Ben found his voice.

"I'm flattered. Of course this catches me by surprise. It's an honor to be considered."

"Well, clearly you're a rising star, Ben, and I do believe you're up to the task. I will need to spend the next year grooming you for the position. We'll talk about that process. But I don't have any question, Ben, about your excelling in the position."

Stunned, Ben sat up taller in his chair. "Thank you for your confidence. Let me give this some thought, if that's okay. When do you need an answer?"

"I would love to make the recommendation within the month. Talk to Claire and see how she feels about becoming the first lady." He chuckled, amused by his own joke.

"Thank you."

"Ben, we'd love to have you."

Claire was off and running.

That always worked well. Being quiet and alone with her thoughts often felt tormenting, so, as usual, she had composed a long list of errands and tasks that would take her out and about. By ten a.m., she had already checked off almost half of her to-dos.

Mid-morning, Claire stopped at her favorite coffee shop to pick up her usual skinny latte, but this time she didn't hop back in her car. Instead, she found herself sitting at a table in the back. She had told herself she needed to check over her errand list, but in fact, she never even pulled it out. She just sat there, sipping, alone with her thoughts and feelings.

Something had started to shift inside her—she could feel it. Sure, many of her raw emotions toward Ben were still there and still stinging, but watching him cry during the therapy session had truly affected her. She sensed his tears were real, and they revealed to her a different Ben. Claire was beginning to understand how Ben's upbringing had conditioned him against expressing his emotions openly, and seeing such deep emotions spill out of him was powerful to witness.

She still didn't see how she could forgive him for his tryst with Bridgette, but perhaps she was starting to trust him again, just a little, particularly in those moments when he was especially vulnerable.

There was something else, too. Something she was feeling for the first time toward Ben—a new and different way in which he was important to her.

Claire reached for her phone. She wanted to talk this over with Steph, but then she caught herself. She refrained from pressing Steph's speed-dial button. *Maybe this is something I should try to talk about with Ben.*

Claire was putting a healthy salad together when Ben's early entrance startled her.

"Hey, honey . . . " Ben's voice echoed through the house.

She heard him drop his briefcase on the chair in the hallway, and he soon appeared at the entrance to the kitchen. "Have a decent day?" he asked.

"Actually, yes," Claire replied. "I got a lot done. Finally took that carton of books over to the church library. Also, dry cleaning, bank, groceries. . .and I stopped to look at that new camera at Shutterbug. To die for—but way too expensive . . . "

"Ahh," Ben replied.

"How was your day?" Claire asked.

"Good. Real good."

They paused, each searching the air for the right beat in which to insert something. Then they both spoke at once:

"Say—"

"You'll never guess—"

Claire looked up. "Okay, you first."

Ben smiled, nodded. "Well, I got a call today from Dr. Smith."

Claire's heart nearly stopped when she heard his name. She knew that Smith had seen Ben and Bridgette together.

Ben saw the cloud come over Claire's face. "No, it's not about that," he said. "Actually, this is a good thing. A very good thing."

"What is it?"

"Well," Ben said, "Smith wants to groom me for the Department Chair. He's offering it to me."

Claire put down the paring knife on the cutting board, stunned. "Ben, that's terrific."

"I'm honored. It's humbling."

"I'm so proud of you."

"Thanks."

"It's what we dreamed of, way back when."

"I know. But—"

"What?"

Ben paused. "I'm not sure I should take it."

Claire cocked her head toward him, puzzled. "Why not?"

"Well, I thought you and I should talk about it at least. Smith needs to know by the end of the month."

To Claire, this was a different Ben. It was a different *them*. "Okay," she said. "So, let's talk about it."

"You're in the middle of—"

"Dinner can wait." Claire turned down the oven dial, and walked out to the living room.

Ben was surprised. *Dinner can wait?* Okay, he'd go with it. "Wine?" he asked.

"Yes, thank you."

And so they talked.

Ben told Claire about his concern that the new position would be even more consuming than his current one. He didn't want to upset the progress they were making, or make the circumstances that had led him to Bridgette even worse than they already were.

As they talked, Claire sensed that Ben was really torn about this—he wasn't just questioning his new opportunity for her sake;

he was honestly saying that he felt he should be spending more time at home. *More time with her.* And yet, she knew he really wanted the job. "But. . . the job means a lot to you, doesn't it?"

Ben nodded. "Yes, but I think what I've been learning is that I may value this for the wrong reasons."

"Like what?"

"I want it because I think it's prestigious for me—makes me important in the eyes of others. My mother and father." He paused. "And you."

Claire sat silent. In the flash of that moment, she could see how her own need had added to Ben's pressure to prove himself to her. She nodded, blinking back tears.

They stopped talking for a while. Facing each other on the couch, they each started to say something, then paused for lack of the right words.

Eventually, Ben said, "We've talked all this time and I haven't asked you about what you were going to say to me, hours ago."

Claire uttered a wistful laugh, aware of the irony of the circumstance. "I was going to tell you how I spent time alone at the coffee shop today, letting everything wash over me. And I realized something. Something new. About you. Well, about my need for you."

"What's that?" Ben said slowly.

"Well, I'm starting to understand what the therapist has been saying about how I cling to you because I need the security you bring, your work and status. It's hard for me to admit it, but I can see some truth in it. And today, I think I understood something else. I think I need you for something else. I need you for just being there, being here, for me. Not the security of your image but the connection with you. I need you for this, Ben, what we're doing here, right now."

Ben nodded. He was still uncomfortable with all of the

emotions flying around. It would take time for him to get used to it, and maybe he would never get fully comfortable expressing and discussing their emotional lives. But he knew he had to try, and that's exactly what he was doing. He had to admit, this was better. For him. For Claire. For their relationship.

"So," Ben said after a pause, "I now have this incredible job offer that gives me great status and an image of achievement, and you're saying you no longer love me for my status and achievement?"

Claire laughed. "Yep, it's kind of like that."

Ben smiled.

They each looked up at the clock. Somehow it was now nine p.m. and the dinner Claire had left in the oven to stay warm was now a dried, shriveled mess.

For once, Claire didn't care.

## THERAPY

# Softening, Risking, and Reaching

*Mature love says, "I need you because I love you."*
—Erich Fromm

As a therapist, I lead clients through a process of self-discovery. Ultimately though, I can't dictate or force the self-discovery—that's something they need to realize, choices they need to make. Those personal "aha's" might happen earlier in the therapy process or later. And sometimes, sadly, they never happen at all.

While I can't force the self-discovery, I can help clients focus on the keys to it. I believe these keys are *attachment needs* (understanding of the needs that drive our behaviors) and *emotional currency* (the ability to express honestly the deepest emotions we feel). When these are engaged, amazing things often happen.

In the case of Ben and Claire, I had walked them through the valley of attachment needs and emotional currency, and they had achieved some personal breakthroughs, individually and together. At our next therapy session, they came to me talking about these breakthroughs and, in particular, one long evening of conversation they'd shared.

Delighted as I was to hear this, I knew there was more work

to do. If anything, Ben was the one who showed the most progress. He had seemed to get a fix on his emotional distance and avoidance. He was trying to do something about it. His efforts to change were noted by Claire, who was more than eager to embrace his change, even as she was slow to engage in her own.

My goal in this session was to help Claire acknowledge fully her attachment need and let Ben in. This bonding event would give them the capacity to make the difficult choice to make their relationship *primary* in both of their lives.

**Therapist:** Ben has described something—a long conversation—that the two of you experienced together this past week. Claire, do you agree that this was positive and maybe a big step forward? Or do you have a different view of it?

**Claire:** Yes, I agree. It was good. A good step.

**Therapist:** Ben mentioned that, for him, it's been a lot of emotions swirling on the inside. How has it felt to you?

**Claire:** I am swirling on the inside, too. This is such a change from the way Ben has related to me in the past. I do believe now that he is sincere. Though, it is going to take me some time to heal from everything that has happened.

**Therapist:** Of course it will. . . . Claire, I'm interested in the change that happened in you this past week. You came into that evening, that conversation, with something new. Can you describe that for me?

**Claire:** I'm not sure I can. Not sure I understand it myself. But that day, I found myself thinking of Ben, seeing him, differently. I needed him, but this was about needing him in a different way.

**Therapist:** Can you say more about that?

**Claire:** I don't think I understand it myself. I just knew I needed him—and not just the image of him. Something about that was different for me.

**Therapist:** Do you have any idea what prompted this new awareness in you?

**Claire:** No, not exactly. But I know that seeing Ben in our last therapy session—his tears, I mean, and hearing him speak his feelings about me—that touched me. Deeply.

**Therapist:** I think what you're experiencing with this new "need for Ben" is probably at the heart of your attachment issues, Claire. As we've discussed before, you grew up with parents who were unavailable to you as a child. You developed a need for the security and attention that they never provided. As a teenager, your relationships reflected that. And when you married Ben, right from the beginning it was about needing the security and attention that Ben represented to you. Does that make sense?

**Claire:** (*Nodding*) But what is so wrong with that? Don't we all have needs like that going into marriage?

**Therapist:** The problem is that you didn't really need Ben *for Ben*. You needed security and attention and the *image* of Ben. You clung to the things that Ben represented, not who he really is.

**Claire:** And so, the other day, and that night—

**Therapist:** You discovered Ben. The real Ben. (*There is silence in the room. Claire is absorbing this deeply, I can tell. She has tears in her eyes.*)

**Claire:** (*Her voice cracking*) I feel so messed up.

**Therapist:** We all are, Claire. The question is how do we overcome it?

**Claire:** How *do* we overcome it?

**Therapist:** We have to be able to express our deepest, truest feelings to each other.

**Claire:** I think I've always been quick to express my emotions. I've always been frustrated that Ben doesn't.

**Therapist:** Well, I believe Ben is now copping to that, and starting to work on it. But, Claire, I would suggest that the emotions of anger and frustration you are expressing have triggered Ben's insecurity, rather than drawing him close to you. When you took the risk of telling him how hurt and afraid you were of losing him, and how much you need him, he was able to move lovingly toward you.

I went on to talk about the idea of "making your primary primary," the importance of emotional connection with a spouse on a substantial level. Ben and Claire had each made their work—not each other—primary. Claire had been engaging Ben with anger and resentment while covering up her vulnerability, her need to be able to rely on him to respond to her deepest emotional fears and longings. This left Ben feeling as if he could not be enough for Claire, as if he would always disappoint her. It was his confiding in Bridgette about his fears that led to their connection. Ben actually longed to know that Claire still needed him just the way she did when they met. Before ending our session, I wanted to give both Ben and Claire the opportunity to speak to each other on a deep emotional level. This is the basis for effective Emotionally Focused Therapy.

**Therapist:** Claire, you said before that you were starting to trust Ben again. Are you at a place where you could take the risk of letting him know how deeply you love and need him?

**Claire:** (*Hesitates but then slowly nods*) Well, I see his commitment to me, our family. Yes, I am feeling more that I can start to trust him again.

**Therapist:** Claire, what would it be like to turn toward Ben and tell him that you want to trust him again, and that you, too, need to find the connection you have lost? Is that something you think you can do?

(*Claire looks hesitant. There are red blotches on her neck and she is clearly stressed. But she nods that she is willing to do this.*)

**Claire:** (*Turning to Ben*) Ben, I have to say I am overwhelmed by the things you have been saying to me, especially by the feelings you are expressing. I believe they are true. I am starting to trust you again, Ben. (*Voice breaking*) Yes, I want to trust you again. (*Pauses, then in tears*) And until now, I hadn't understood how deeply I have needed you, too!

(*Claire leans toward Ben and he pulls her into him, placing her head on his chest. He holds her while tears stream down his face.*)

These are sacred moments. I have been allowed to be present for an intimate embrace that may well change the rest of their lives. All I can do is sit silently and witness the exchange of grace that feels as if it is flowing from heaven. The minutes that pass seem like an eternity. It is important to savor the meaning in this moment so they can revisit it outside of the session.

**Ben:** Claire, it means a lot to me that you are willing to give me another chance. I see so many things differently now. I don't have all of the answers, but I will do whatever it takes to put our relationship and you in first place.

*(Claire nods and lets in Ben's reassurance as tears continue to roll down her face.)*

There is more work to be done, as their fears will inevitably cause them to recoil, unconsciously, from their newfound depth of connection. They will stumble, pull back, and then step toward each other again. Claire has work to do in opening up her insecure attachment emotions. Ben will have to work constantly at being emotionally present in Claire's life.

But they understand much more clearly now. They are together and deeply connected, perhaps for the first time in their marriage.

17

SCIENCE

# Rescued
# by Connection

*Love is our true destiny. We do not find the meaning
of life by ourselves alone—we find it with another.*
—Thomas Merton, *Love and Living*

The genius of Emotionally Focused Therapy is in its healing of the insecure emotions of disconnected couples. The goal is to rescue each person from the fear that threatens to destroy the marriage. The EFT approach helps couples communicate their terror in a way that encourages each to respond to the other with compassion rather than contempt.

After years of careful observation of emotional communication with couples in crisis, Drs. Johnson and Greenberg discovered that there are specific steps for rescuing relationships.[23] These sequential steps apply to all relationships in crisis, regardless of the reason for the conflict. They are powerful emotional interventions that help couples rewire their brains and bypass the destructive habitual arguments that destroy relationships.

There are three stages of EFT that help couples move from crisis to deep connection. EFT therapists spend years of training and supervision of video taped sessions to become certified in this model. EFT therapists know where couples are on the map of change and do not move them into deeper emotional connection until they are ready.

## Escaping the Cycle

The first stage of EFT is *cycle de-escalation*. The majority of couples who come in for therapy are caught in a negative cycle of emotional conflict that feels unique to them. Regardless of what they are arguing about, they find themselves in a familiar pattern of arguing that nearly always leaves them feeling disconnected and alone. The argument about the burned toast becomes heated because of years of accusation and defensiveness that spark and ignite the conflict. By understanding how to express their vulnerable emotions, and not fire back defensive responses, couples can learn how to escape the cycle.

As we discussed earlier, the majority of couples in conflict polarize and adopt two very different ways of coping with relationship struggles. EFT therapists use the terms *pursuer* and *withdrawer* to describe these positions. In most cases, pursuers are female and withdrawers are male, though the opposite is sometimes the case. Relationships with two withdrawers can find themselves immobilized. Rarely do you find two pursuers in a relationship.

When pursuers feel insecure, they express their emotions in an attempt to gain emotional reassurance from their partners. They want to know that their partner feels as deeply about an issue as they do. If their partner does not respond with emotional authenticity and accurately mirror their emotions, the pursuer becomes even more insecure, trying again, with even more emotional intensity to get the point across. The expectation is that *more* emotion will surely pull at the heartstrings of their beloved. If the lack of emotional response persists, the pursuer often expresses *attacking emotion and exasperation* to try to get the withdrawer to engage. The conflict escalates.

Withdrawers become immobilized when confronted by their pursuing partner's heightened emotion. They tend to be uncomfortable expressing—or even feeling—emotion in the first place. Withdrawers often try to come across as unaffected by the emotion aimed at them. In the withdrawer's mind, expressing emotion will only make the situation worse. He (or she—but probably he, so we will use the male pronoun here) may be afraid that if he allows himself to express his feelings, an angry outburst could result. In most cases he feels overwhelmed and does not know how to use emotion to respond to the angry protest of his pursuing partner.

This pursuer-withdrawer dynamic creates the perfect storm in nearly every troubled relationship. The pursuer's emotional flooding, or overload, causes the withdrawer to almost automatically flee rather than fight for the relationship. This pushes the primitive panic button in the pursuer. Pursuers must see their partner's emotion. They must know that their withdrawing partner cares emotionally about their deep pain. If this does not happen, the pursuit will continue on and on.

Couples caught in this negative cycle of interaction repeatedly fall into the same pattern of conflict. This is confusing, painful, and fear producing. In time, the smallest disagreement can send them into the spiral of another negative cycle. When this happens, rather than giving each other the emotional reassurance necessary to restore intimacy, each person defends why he or she is hurting the other.

Ben and Claire's coping strategies were not unique. Ben was a withdrawer and Claire a pursuer. Claire's anxious pursuit and Ben's withdrawal continued even after the patterns had been defined in their therapy sessions. Claire continued to bombard Ben with texts and phone calls when her insecurities were triggered. Ben knew that ignoring or running from her pleas to be heard were not what Claire needed—but, when fired upon, he continued to default to his finely tuned emotionless response.

The cycle is driven by unacknowledged vulnerable emotions, most of which are based on the couple's fears of losing the relationship. One would think it would be so simple for people who love each other to simply acknowledge how afraid they are of losing each other. Nothing could be further from the truth. When we are afraid of losing love, we instinctively move into a posture of self-protection. This only validates our partner's fear that we really do not care. *Our self-protection escalates our partner's fear.*

De-escalation is about helping a couple see their own emotional cycle of conflict. When they see what each of them are doing to trigger the cycle, they become empowered to stop the destructive dance. Pursuers usually trigger withdrawers by blaming. Withdrawers trigger pursuers by silence and invalidating facial expressions. A monotone verbal response can send a triggering message to an angry pursuer that her partner does not care.

Withdrawing men sometimes need to learn to identify their emotions before they can express them. Even though their voice tones and facial expressions give them away, they are often unaware of what they are really feeling. It takes time for them to connect discomfort in their chest with fear or a pain in their gut with anger. With time and the help of a skilled therapist, they can learn to make the connection between discomfort in their body and the actual emotions they are feeling.

It is this lack of emotional awareness that makes their emotionally hurt pursuing wives feel crazy with frustration. They interpret their husband's lack of emotional responsiveness as their not caring about their feelings. The truth is that they cannot show emotional compassion about their partner's emotions when they cannot feel their own emotions. It is not enough for them to say they are sorry. They must express that they are sorry with emotion if the apology is going to heal the pursuer's hurt.

Withdrawers have often spent a lifetime disconnecting from their emotions. It takes time for them to both recognize what they are feeling and then express feeling for their partner who they have emotionally injured. They feel stupid and awkward learning how to feel their own and their partner's emotions. Acknowledging that they struggle and need help with emotional communication takes courage. If they feel disrespected because they struggle with emotional communication, they may never learn to open up.

Feeling understood and safe in the therapy environment is critical to the couple's progress toward escaping the negative cycle. The therapist expresses care and understanding for each partner's frustration with the process. The therapist helps partners to understand the other person's love and attachment longings.

When each person can stop reacting, attacking or withdrawing the negative cycle is deactivated. This is done by letting go of accusations and by simply expressing the vulnerable emotions they are each feeling. Each partner feels loved and understood when their emotions are mirrored back to them.

The first stage of EFT is about creating the safety they need in order to acknowledge their fear of relationship loss. Once the couple can see the cycle and acknowledge their fearful emotions, they can begin a new dance. This dance is all about reassuring each other and pulling each other close when fear is aroused.

## Deepening and Forgiving

In this second stage, now with a clear understanding of the negative cycle, the Emotionally Focused Therapist helps each person identify and more fully express their disowned attachment emotions, needs, and self-perceptions. Expressing these deep hidden struggles creates the opportunity for the forbidden places of pain to be understood and cared for. We unconsciously keep ourselves in cycles of painful conflict by not acknowledging and expressing our attachment fears, shame struggles, and needs for validation.

With a de-escalated cycle, the transforming stage-two work can be started. Many people have never had a safe love relationship that allowed them to talk about their insecurities. Each person learns how to invite their partner to safely talk about the emotional injuries caused by themselves or another person. The listening person responds with compassion and understanding. These vulnerable and validating conversations are deeply moving. It is not uncommon for one person to hold the other with tearful expressions of gratitude of finally feeling understood.

This creates the foundation for forgiveness. In love relationships, forgiveness is a process that requires an emotional and not just an intellectual confession. When the offending partner feels safe and loved, it frees him or her to express the remorse of betrayal. When the injured person feels the sincerity of the partner's emotional confession, it releases their hold on emotional resentment.

True emotional forgiveness in love relationships requires this heart-level exchange of needs and wants. It is simply too dangerous to forgive a lover who will not confess his or her deep emotional need for love. With the heart-level assurance of need in place, transgressions that surpass comprehension can be forgiven. Compassion for any crime is possible when viewed through the eyes of loving attachment. Fragile attachment bonds are strengthened and new attachment bonds are formed when needs are expressed and accepted and attachment injuries are forgiven.

The stage-two process of compassionately hearing each other's hurts and failures deepens the relationship and forms new emotional bonds. It frees each person to have a more secure view of self and of their partner, creating an overall improvement in self-esteem and identity.

EFT therapists often find themselves quoting Sue Johnson's coined truth: "*We find ourselves in the arms of another.*" Unlike the popular notion that we find our identity alone, the stage-two therapy work teaches couples that they grow as individuals by depending on each other for emotional support and validation. As each person in the relationship feels the safety of emotional compassion, this new dance creates the opportunity for *forgiveness,* and *deepening* the relationship by creating bonding experiences. Old hurts are healed and we achieve new capacity to become our best. Couples learn to acknowledge and express fearful emotions as they come up. They no longer waste energy trying to repress their emotional pain. They learn that their loving relationship is the best place to find healing and understanding. This creates the foundation for intimacy and a sustained feeling of closeness and being cared for.

Like magic, our perception of our life partner transforms as our hearts make room for the pain they hold. We stop seeing the other person through the critical lens of perfection. Behaviors that were once an irritant become opportunities for us to show compassion and provide comfort.

Most of us live in cultures that discourage neediness. Couples learn in stage-two work that *we are only as needy as our unmet need.* Meeting the need that we are referring to here requires another person. As we learn to allow ourselves to need and meet our partner's need for emotional love and support, we become less clingy and more secure.

It is very moving to watch a couple express their deep love and need for each other in therapy. It is a deeply spiritual moment when the souls of two people open, perhaps for the first time, to the love they so desperately need for wholeness.

In this beautiful opening of hearts, the withdrawing partner expresses the loneliness and fear behind the wall of silence. The blaming pursuer, in amazement, sees the likeness in her fears and loneliness. The pursuer's heated anger calms. Her sharp, accusing tone of voice becomes soft and supportive. The withdrawer discovers fresh energy to initiate in the relationship. The pursuer finds new safety in this initiation and is able to trust in those promptings. It's like the world that was spinning chaotically out-of-control is set right on its axis. Each partner finds a home in the other, and is able to live into their fullness.

When couples make this stage-two shift into deep acceptance of self and other, they have a newfound capacity to face struggles together. The fear of having different opinions fades and the conversation about different points of view opens exciting possibilities for new learning, without the fear of rejection. The only thing that is non-negotiable is the love that they have for each other.

It should be no surprise that completing stage-two work is the best predictor of long-term love relationship stability. It is difficult to get knocked off course when the bond is deep and the attachment is secure. This kind of profound emotional connection is more than a temporary feeling. It is a sustaining life-giving force that is at the foundation of well-being and forward movement.

## Making Your Primary Primary

The third stage of EFT is where the consolidation and integration takes place. I call this *making your primary primary*. This stage is about lining up your life priorities so that the attachment is kept secure and growing. Staying emotionally connected takes time and attention. Relationships become unhealthy, just like bodies do, when they are not exercised. Modern life presents us with a wide array of choices for each person in the relationship to become productive and grow. The choices we make can either deepen or weaken our love relationships.

The jobs we choose, when we start a family, how we manage money, how we vacation, how we work out, our hobbies and our spiritual direction all have the potential for creating closeness and distance. Sex is not automatic. It takes energy and attention to keep a sex life alive for the long run. The lack of a regular, mutually satisfying sex life is a sure sign of attachment injury, or priorities being out of balance.

Lasting structural changes in a relationship are only possible when broken attachment bonds have been healed and renewed. Too often, couples in therapy are challenged to make behavioral changes before they have the emotional security necessary to make a sustainable change. When attachment bonds are broken, gifts, flowers, romantic dinners, and exotic vacations will only create temporary closeness. Behavioral gestures of love are signs of responsiveness when the emotional co-regulation is working. When there is hurt and a lack of forgiveness, these gestures are experienced as manipulation or placating. The same flowers that will warm the heart of a securely attached wife may anger her when she feels distant and damaged after an act of relationship betrayal. Knowing your partner's language of love will not repair a relationship that is not connected.

It can, however, be remarkably easy to make major structural changes in a relationship once emotional intimacy is flowing. In the third stage of EFT, the couple is encouraged to have conversations about the issues that keep them from enjoying the depth of connection they both desire. What previously felt like power and control debates are now conversations about how to create a connected lifestyle.

This is the transformative work of *making your primary primary*. When each person understands the primary importance of their attachment bond, all life choices are evaluated through this lens. Individuals who are attachment-aware monitor and maintain healthy closeness with their beloved. They know when their "love buckets" are low and they feel safe in asking for a refill. And like Ben, they may turn down career promotions that threaten the health of their relationship.

Couples who make their primary primary understand the incredible challenges of raising children. They are careful to stay connected and in alliance so that they can lovingly parent while minimizing mixed messages. They support each other in front of their children and work out differences behind closed doors. They teach their children to come to them with their needs for attention rather than acting out for attention.

Making our primary primary in adult life is about giving our adult love relationships the priority and power to transform our lives. When we make our primary primary, we heal our past, present, and future. As we place our relationship with our partner above any other, we protect and create safe space for our attachment bond to heal and transform our lives. Even insecure childhood attachment bonds can be healed in the warmth and acceptance of a loving, attached adult relationship.

It is helpful for couples to think of their relationship as an epicenter for the nourishment of their deepest needs, wants, and capacity for transforming growth. There is no other relationship like the primary relationship, which offers the opportunity for total transparency and deep mirroring of emotion. This emotional support and feedback is the primary way that we come to understand ourselves. Feeling grounded and confident allows us to be ourselves in our work and social relationships. Our primary relationship is of utmost importance to our identity, health and sense of wellbeing.

When any relationship other than our primary one becomes

more trusted and relied upon, our primary relationship suffers injury or even destruction. Therefore, how we structure our lives to secure and protect our primary relationship is of vital importance. We learn to express our emotional needs to our partner. Sharing with others without appropriate boundaries in place creates the possibility for a competing emotional connection that can weaken or destroy our primary love relationship.

Like Ben and Claire, couples that stop making their primary primary eventually will find themselves in crisis. Unmet needs build unconsciously, and we become hooks for others who are under-nurtured or under-affirmed. Work relationships often fall prey to these deep primal needs for connection. In today's progressive culture, where men and women work closely together in surgery suites, corporate suites, academia, and even on the battlefield, there is ample opportunity for the triggering of our bonding emotions by someone outside of the primary relationship.

Throughout this book we have attempted to provide our readers with the story and science of what builds and weakens relationships. As we've shown, the problems may well have started as early as the first years of life. The attachment failures that occur before two people come together often have an impact on their primary adult love relationship. This shows up with misplaced priorities and negative cycle conflicts. With enough years of emotional disconnection, the couple is ripe to be picked off by an emotional or physical affair.

Even when an affair has happened, as devastating as it is, it is simply naive to blame the crisis exclusively on the person who strayed. There is always a bigger story that needs to be understood and insecurities that need to be healed. The cost of being human requires us to live in the vulnerable position of needing to give and receive love. No one can survive long in love deprivation without eventually failing self or others.

When a relationship crisis happens to us, it is a wake-up opportunity to dig in and understand how we are made and what we truly need to survive and thrive. By learning to see and escape their negative cycle, by deepening and forgiving and by making their primary primary, couples can discover the reality that a lifetime of secure love is waiting to be realized. With secure attachment as a foundation, much of what troubles us disappears, leaving us with renewed strength to take on life's challenges together.

## STORY

# Epilogue

*Love is composed of a single soul*
*inhabiting two bodies.*
–Aristotle

B en awakened on Saturday morning to sun shining on the deck and the sound of birds ushering in springtime. Both kids had weekend plans away from home. Ben had talked with Claire about a special weekend alone—a B&B on a lake and a short drive into wine country. He wondered if they could get through a day, let alone two, without falling into their familiar cycle of fighting. They would try.

Ben was learning in therapy that he needed to stay emotionally present to Claire, and he was trying his best. It wasn't easy, though. He knew now that he had been shaped in childhood to distance himself from emotions, so that in adulthood he lacked the skills to express them easily. Opening himself up to Claire emotionally felt awkward at best, exhausting for sure. Still, he knew it was something he had to work hard to do.

The previous few weeks had been some of the most challenging in Claire's life. She had learned that Ben actually did have feelings. Seeing him display them in the therapist's office had shocked her. Even in their early days of courting, he'd never appeared so vulnerable. He had expressed love with words back then, but she'd never really been sure those words reflected real emotion. Now, he seemed different. He was really reaching deep to unearth his true feelings and share them with her.

Weeks had passed since Claire had checked Ben's cell phone for text messages to or from Bridgette. At first, this was intentional on her part, an act of will. She knew she had to begin to trust again, as difficult as that seemed. Ben had said that it was over, and she knew she had to let that seep into her heart and become her new reality. But, what started as a discipline—not checking Ben's phone—at some point became Claire's new norm. For the past week or so, she simply hadn't thought about it.

The therapist had told them that the path forward required each of them to make intentional choices about expressing true emotions and daring to trust again. There would be fits and starts; progress would be incremental. But there would be progress. Claire had seen some changes in Ben as well as in herself.

Claire began to stir as she heard Ben grinding the coffee. It felt so awkward to be alone in the house with her husband. The kids had always been there. She couldn't remember the last time the two of them had gotten away alone. Claire thought ahead to the B&B they had reserved. She wished now that Ben had chosen something less intimate. For all the good things happening between them, it was as if they were strangers getting to know each other for the first time. A Marriott would feel safer to her for their first weekend away in so many years.

Ben bustled about in the kitchen, steering clear of the thoughts that could easily surface. The two-hour car ride, the romantic room on the lake, the wine they would share over a quiet dinner . . . it could easily panic him if he allowed it to. So he stuffed it and prepared breakfast, remembering how much Claire had loved to be surprised like this in the old days.

He was startled when she came into the kitchen in her bathrobe just as he was putting Danish on a tray. Without a word, she grabbed two plates and a knife and a couple of mugs. Ben grabbed the paper from the doorstep and separated it into the sections each of them liked to start with, and for a little while, they slipped into their silent worlds. This was a comfortable place for both of them.

The day was gorgeous and not to be wasted, so they were behind the wheel by nine a.m. Just as Google Maps had promised, after two hours they were meandering down the long tree-lined drive leading to the B&B—which turned out to be a rather spectacular Victorian manse. Ben had selected it and Claire was impressed.

Ben took a deep breath as the owners welcomed them and ushered them into the quaint, romantic bedroom on the second floor. The queen-sized bed seemed half the size as their familiar king. He wished he could bring to mind his early years with Claire. He knew that there was a time when just thinking of having Claire alone in this room would have brought chills down his spine. He wondered if Claire was as nervous as he was.

The floral fabric put a smile on Claire's tense face. She couldn't have chosen a more lovely room. *Please, God, let this be a restart for us. Be with us as we fumble through this maze.*

They put down their overnight cases and began to look around. The bathroom was small but tidy and immaculate. The little fireplace would be cozy later on, when the temperature dropped.

Feeling unusually hungry, Claire was pleased that the proprietors had set out a light buffet upon their arrival. She smiled when Ben waxed chivalrous and said, "Well, my lady, shall we see what awaits for lunch?" She took his hand for the first time in months.

As they made their way to the dining room, their Downton Abbey role-playing was a useful distraction from the awkwardness they each were feeling.

Lunchtime passed pleasantly as they got to know the owners of the B&B, an older couple who seemed to love the life of hospitality. This became a welcome distraction for both Ben and Claire, each of whom was realizing desperately that they didn't really know how to navigate this time alone together, to do the work of true connection.

After giving them a brief tour of the place, the proprietors left them alone, and Ben and Claire decided to walk down by the lake. There they found Adirondack chairs and sat side by side for a long while without saying a word.

Finally, Ben spoke up. "So . . . what are you feeling?"

Claire thought for a moment. "It's beautiful here."

"No," Ben replied. And swallowing hard, he added, "What are you *feeling*? About *me*."

Claire spoke slowly, calmly. "I feel really awkward. Like I'm getting to know you for the first time."

"I know. Me too. It's like things are different now, at least a little, but in a really good way. But I feel afraid of going back to before."

"Yes, I know," Claire said. "Me too." She paused, looking over at Ben. "But maybe . . . you know . . . we don't have to go back. To before . . ."

Ben nodded. "Maybe we don't."

A sailboat drifted into their view, then angled away toward the horizon.

"Lakes always feel peaceful to me," Claire said. "And hopeful."

"You know," Ben said, "as a kid, I loved to skip stones across the lake. I used to think it was possible to skip a stone in such a way that it would never stop."

189

Claire laughed. "So some are still skipping?"

"Maybe so," Ben said with a smile.

Somehow the plans they'd made for the afternoon—wine-tastings and a chamber concert—fell away, forgotten. Hours later, Ben and Claire were still sitting in the Adirondack chairs, still talking. Not about work and kids for a change, but about their lake experiences as kids, about Ben's fear of snakes, Claire's addiction to salt water taffy one teenage summer, Ben's miserable failure at basketball in high school. They spent a full hour comparing recurring dreams they'd had as kids and again sometimes as adults. Ben even found himself telling Claire that there were times he felt ambivalent about being a doctor.

It didn't have to be on a lake or near wine country or at a cozy Victorian B&B. It didn't have to be on a romantic getaway. This conversation—this experience—could have happened anywhere. Having lost all sense of time and place, Ben and Claire found themselves *being themselves with each other.*

Later that day, things would become awkward again, though less so and more briefly. They didn't fight, but dinner at a restaurant turned out to be distracting and superficial. They found themselves connecting once again during an evening drive through a moonlit valley, only to fall back into awkward silence on their way back to the B&B.

That night, Claire crawled into bed and pulled the down comforter up to her chin. She had chosen a nightgown that was somewhere between flannels and silk. She was scared at the thought that she was sleeping with a man she kind of knew but didn't; a man who had betrayed her but had come back; a man who was now trying hard to be *her man.*

Ben got ready for bed in the bathroom, filled with thoughts

from the day. Something had happened between them, something good and hopeful. For some hours, sharing himself with her wasn't so demanding. It was fun, even. This gave him hope.

Ben slid into bed beside his wife. With lights off, he simply touched Claire's fingertips before closing his gentle grasp around her hand. Cautiously, he pulled her to his chest and held her.

Claire felt secure for the first time in months.

Together, they drifted off into sleep, slipping into dreams of one single stone skipping forever.

# Conclusion

The Final Prayer of Jesus:
*". . . that they may be one as we are one."*
—John 17:22 (NIV)

Couples generally come to a therapist when some trauma—an affair, marital battle, family tragedy—has hit and caused conflict between them. They're looking to fix what happened. What they seldom realize is that the event that triggered this "crisis" is just the tsunami wave hitting the beach. It was actually caused by fault lines in their relationship that had begun forming long before they'd even met. Every significant relationship creates emotional memory that makes attachment natural or difficult in adult love relationships.

Attachment theory simply says to a couple that their relationship is governed by childhood needs for security and attention, needs carried into adulthood and eventually played out in marriage. The conditions are set for cyclical arguments and disconnection when a man or woman enters a lifelong love relationship with an insecure attachment style. The more the emotional disconnection, the greater the chances that one or the other person will seek comfort outside of the relationship. Betrayal is sometimes the final straw that sets the tsunami in motion.

Much of the cause of these relational issues has to do with cognitive approaches to family and child rearing that held sway during a particular era in our history—an emphasis on rational behaviors at the expense of emotional expression. We are, to some degree, victims of the parenting styles our parents learned and employed while raising us. The result is several generations of men and women who have deep emotional needs and little means to openly and fully express them.

This is the problem.

Ben and Claire are emblematic of many, many couples in the world today. While they may not be a perfect match to you and your marriage, no doubt many aspects of their behaviors and relationship ring true.

For Ben and Claire, and for you, there is hope. It's found in a therapeutic process that heals insecure attachment by focusing on the emotional fears and needs in the adult love relationship. Couples heal present-past as each person learns to authentically express, mirror, and support the emotions of the other. Old emotional memory is replaced as each person has the new experience of having his or her emotional fears and needs understood and validated.

It is critical that you understand that the courtship passion and sexual desire of the early marriage years naturally subside—as they are largely a chemical response triggered by new love. The challenge of meaningful adult relationships is to find true connection beyond that, through emotional connection.

Further, couples need to be aware that they can easily become "committed to commitment"—which becomes a roadblock of its own kind. Commitment by itself will not maintain and grow a relationship. Being committed to lifetime emotional connection is the key to relationship growth and security. We cannot mentally muscle ourselves through a disconnected relationship.

The pain of disconnection makes us vulnerable to anxiety, depression, health problems, addictions, and betrayals. Learning to create secure emotional connection must be our first priority.

These three things—the negative cycle, the waning of intimate desire, and the failure to make our primary relationship primary—are warning sirens that the tsunami will strike if the emotional attachment is not repaired.

We believe that even couples with early life relationship trauma can repair insecure emotions by understanding the big picture of what creates lifelong love. In some cases, couples need to work with a therapist who can help them heal their damaged emotional memory by experiencing the nurture and support of their current love relationship. This pathway to inner peace is available to all who seek it.

This is the promise.

We are passionate about helping people realize successful emotional connection in their relationships. We trust this book has helped you come closer to that promise.

Michael and Paula Regier

# Discussion Questions

Learning how to grow emotional connection is a process of learning how to apply the science of attachment to day-to-day life. The following discussion questions can guide you through reflection and discussion of the key concepts in this book.

These questions are designed to help you make positive relationship changes by understanding and identifying with the characters in the book. The questions will help you put yourself in Ben and Claire's shoes and learn with them about how to repair and strengthen a relationship. As you resonate and problem-solve with them, you will be finding your own answers.

We do not provide any "right answers" here because in most cases, there is no one right answer when it comes to relationships. Should new moms work or stay at home? How much should career be a priority? How should couples parent together? It all depends. Each relationship is different. The attachment science we've provided in this book is fairly definitive, but applying it effectively depends on the abilities and needs of each couple.

This is why discussion is so important. Try not to give advice or judge others for the choices or comments they are making. It is difficult for any of us to understand the challenges faced by others. Coming back to the science and allowing others to own their way of coming to terms with it is the best way to support them.

A note to couples who are already experiencing conflict in their relationship: If there is active or unhealed betrayal or if your cycle of arguing is easily triggered, you may need to work with a therapist in addition to going through this material. If you are triggered in a group discussion, save the processing of your hurt for your therapy session.

Not all couples therapists understand how to work with attachment emotion. Finding a therapist trained in Emotionally Focused Therapy is the best way to facilitate what you are learning in this book. The International Center for Excellence in Emotionally Focused Therapy http://eft.ca/ has a list of EFT therapists located all over the world.

We are continuing to develop resources, seminars, and online learning opportunities for couples and groups who want to learn from their experience. Go to http://www.michaelregier.com/ for further resources and learning opportunities.

## Part One
## Broken Promises: Blindsided by Betrayal

### 1. What is new relationship fantasy and reality?

*Claire soaked in the memory. Her smart and handsome Ben had swept her off her feet. They had embraced life, running toward everything it held for them. They were the perfect couple, compatible and rarely arguing. They meticulously carved out their future . . . together. Partners for life! Those had been the three sweetest words of their vows.*

- Are new relationships truly wonderful or are the memories that we construct about them part of some kind of fantasy we create and keep?

- How common is it for people in committed relationships to form their best memories in their first years together?

## 2.  What does new love talk look like?

*"Steph, you can't imagine the messages. I scrolled backwards and there were dozens of them. They were so intimate . . . kind of steamy, Steph. It was like reading a romance novel." Claire sobbed between words. "They talked like Ben and I used to, years ago—like teenagers in love. It's been forever since he's said those things to me, or even felt them, probably."*

- What do you think of how Ben was expressing himself to Claire?
- Was this behavior unique to Ben, or something that happens to most people in new love relationships?
- What does this say about Ben's love for Claire? Is it the real thing?

## 3.  How does emotional connection protect relationships?

*"I've begged him for years to let me into his world, and now he's sharing himself with another woman. Why her? Why couldn't he give me a chance?"* Claire remembered the countless fights where she had pleaded with him to show some emotion, to let her know how he actually felt about things, to respond to her. He had been quick to share his thoughts, but never his feelings.

- Why do you think Claire begged Ben for years to share his feelings with her?
- What do you think made it easier for Ben to share his feelings with another woman?

## 4.  Why does relationship trauma cause hypervigilance?

[Claire has been traumatized by Ben's affair and now is hyper-vigilant. She has lost all trust in Ben and is constantly looking for signs of betrayal.]

*"I'm sorry, Claire. I don't get it. I just don't understand why you can't trust me. We can't live like this. I can't be falsely accused every time another woman crosses my field of vision. That's not going to work for either of us."*

- Why is Claire hypervigilant?
- How can Ben help her heal?

> ## Part Two
> ## Relationship Trauma:
> ## Face to Face With Our Enemies

## 5.  What is an affair?

Ben: *Wait a second, wait a second. This is . . . I told you, Claire, I have not had an affair. I did not cross a sexual boundary.*

- How do you define an *affair*?

## 6.  Why does forgiveness require emotional expression?

Therapist: *So it feels like your whole world is falling apart right now and you're melting down on the inside. You just want Ben to understand the magnitude of what he has done.*

- How will Claire know when Ben does understand the magnitude of what he has done, and why is this important?

## 7.  Why are many people blindsided by an affair?

Claire: *I was terrified. I was so confused. How did this happen?*

Therapist: (Repeating her words back to her) *"How did this happen?" "I can't believe it." "How could this happen to us?"*

Claire: (Taking a deep breath) *Yeah, how could this happen to us?*

- Why is it that most couples can't imagine that they could be vulnerable to an affair?

## 8. What are healthy relationship boundaries?

Ben: *You have to understand, Claire. We worked together. We were in training together. You have to understand that people who work together get close. They talk about their lives and they get close. And yes, we got very, very close.*

- Do you think Ben's relationship boundaries were healthy or unhealthy?

## 9. What causes an attack cycle in relationships?

Therapist: *So for you, Claire, it kind of feels like your foundations have been rocked. You feel unsafe. You just don't know where you stand anymore.*

Claire: *Yes, exactly.*

Therapist: *So, Ben, when Claire talks about how she is overwhelmed and doesn't know where she stands with you, what happens to you when you hear that?*

Ben: (Exasperated, raising his voice) *That's it! Now I'm pissed. Here we go again. I feel like she's just constantly attacking me and she's suspicious of everything I do. It feels like I can't do anything right. I just don't—I don't know what to do. I'm just getting really angry about her always accusing me of betraying her.*

- Why is Claire attacking, and how can Ben help her heal?

## 10. How do kids and career affect connection?

Therapist: *So, what happens to you, Ben, when you hear how much Claire wanted a deeper connection with you? When you hear how hard and how long she tried to reach you before giving up?*

Ben: *Well, it didn't seem like she was very interested in me. It just felt like she was so involved with the kids and with her career . . . It felt like she was always entertaining other women and doing stuff for other people. Frankly, I felt shut down sexually over the years. More and more and more, like she wasn't even that interested in me. So I don't even know what to say when she says that she wanted a more intimate relationship with me.*

- What challenges do kids and career bring to a marriage relationship?

## 11. What are normal attachment needs?

Therapist: *Okay, so for you, Claire, you really needed him to be present to your deepest emotions. You needed him to be compassionate with you and to let you know that he understood when you were struggling with all of the pressures of life and motherhood.*

- Is Claire too needy or is this normal?

## 12. How do outside friendships help and hurt love relationships?

Claire: *Well, he was always at work. I will say this: Ben's been an amazing provider. He's taken such good care of our family, financially that is. He spent hours and hours and hours at work, taking care of his patients. He didn't have time for us by the time he got home. He didn't have time for the kids, for me. He was drained. So I backed off a little. I actually felt kind of sorry for him. Maybe it wasn't reasonable to expect anything from someone who has given it all to someone else...to his patients. So I found support in other relationships. I have a sister who is like my best friend. Stephanie and I spend a lot of time together.*

- How do friendships hinder or help marriage relationships?

### 13. How does trauma affect relationship recovery?

*Trauma is caused by a physical wound or a deeply distressing or life threatening emotional experience. Emotional trauma can be more difficult to overcome than physical trauma. Most of us will never witness our loved ones being swept to their deaths in a tsunami. But many have, or will, experience seemingly less extraordinary emotional events that leave a devastating mark all the same. Emotional trauma should not be taken lightly. It can cause problems that last weeks, years, or even a lifetime. It can be, in psychological terms, an emotional tsunami.*

- How do you think that trauma affects relationship recovery?

### 14. How do healthy families emotionally communicate?

*Many of us grew up with parents who were not comfortable with emotional communication. We were often made to feel ashamed of showing our emotions.*

- What does healthy emotional communication in families look like?

### 15. How do accusations create conflict?

*Claire has overwhelming feelings of emptiness, sadness, and anger. She desperately needs Ben to respond to these emotions with compassion and comfort. Like Claire, many of us express our feelings of deep hurt in the form of accusations. This causes the person who has hurt us to protest in self-defense rather than respond to our hurt with compassion. Claire's anger and accusations toward Ben caused him to feel helpless shame, which he expressed with excuses.*

- How do Claire's accusations cause the opposite response in Ben than she is looking for?

## Part Three
## Early Childhood:
## How Parents Shape Childhood Attachment

### 16. Why do we plead for connection?

*Why hadn't her mother found the time to hold her more, to be cheek-to-cheek with her on her lap? Claire vividly remembered the insatiable need she'd had to be with her mother. She had followed closely on her mother's heels, pleading for attention. The more she was ignored, the louder her demands got. And the harder she tried to be good enough.*

- How did Claire's pleading in childhood relate to her pleading with Ben?

### 17. What is emotional flooding?

*Ben was annoyed by Claire's pursuit. To him, her wildly swinging emotions were an impossible maze to navigate. He didn't grow up that way.*

- What do you think happens in Ben's brain and emotions when Claire pursues him this way?

### 18. Why do relationships require repetitive repentance?

*Therapist: I can just imagine what it was like for you, Ben, to feel like you were at a breaking point. You were so overwhelmed by your own regret that you uncharacteristically erupted with an emotional apology. But now it feels like you two should return to the logical, normal dialogue you are both used to. Am I right that that moment of emotion was uncomfortable for you? How did you feel?*

- Do you think Ben's one-time emotional apology should have been enough to heal Claire's attachment-betrayal injury?

## 19. Why do infants need connection to survive and thrive?

*Infants are unable to survive without the loving, emotional attention of an adult. Emotions are the language infants use to let their caretakers know how they are feeling and needing.*

- What do you think about this statement? Do you believe it?

## 20. How does infant imprinting affect adult relationship security?

*Being secure in the world and living without fear and anxiety is foundational. Yet we are born into an imperfect world with parents who carry their own deep fears and insecurities about love. Our early experiences with our parents place an imprint on our brains that we carry for the rest of our lives.*

- How did the ways in which Ben and Claire grew up affect their adult love relationship?

## 21. How do insecure attachment styles create conflict?

*On the surface, both Ben and Claire looked as if they had model parents. Their material needs were well met, and both were adorable in appearance. But they were both insecurely attached as children and remained so as adults.*

- Ainsworth discovered three different attachment styles in the infants she studied: *Secure, Anxious* and *Avoidant*. Which attachment styles did Ben and Claire have?
- Why do these two attachment styles fuel the fire of conflict?
- Which of those three attachment styles describe you?

## 22. How do shame and guilt affect intimacy?

*Shame is the unspeakable disappointment with self. Shame is fear-based and is usually a reaction to hurt. It causes children to question their integrity or worthiness, and makes us feel bad or wrong about having basic needs and wants. It causes us to feel that we are bad, stupid, or a failure.*

*Shame is different from guilt. Guilt is remorse about having done something that hurts someone else. Shame is feeling bad about who we are rather than about what we have done. Shame can cause a whole range of emotional and relationship problems that impact us for the rest of our lives.*

- Give an example of how shame and guilt are different.

- How do shame and guilt affect intimacy?

## Part Four
## New Love: Attraction's Fantasy
## and the Chemistry of New Love

### 23. Why does new love emotion fade?

*The reality was, at first Claire had rocked Ben's world. She was beautiful and intelligent without needing to show it off. She had a heartbreaking smile. She really did intoxicate me. He hyper-focused on finding ways to steal her affections. She had a way of making him feel she was off-limits while pulling him toward her at the same time. She made me crazy.*

- Why didn't Claire's euphoric emotional impact on Ben last?

### 24. What causes fatal attractions?

*Claire used her sexuality to attract guys—especially those that blew hot and cold or were indifferent.*

- What caused Claire to be attracted to men who blew hot and cold?

## 25. Why do feelings of abandonment surface?

*Somehow, all those years ago, Claire had felt that Ben, too, would abandon her. Now, she was feeling that total fear of abandonment once again.*

- Claire struggled with feelings of abandonment in her early relationships and again when Ben had the affair. What do you think kept her from feeling this way for the majority of the time she was with him?

## 26. What causes affair infatuation?

*But it was soon clear that Mike had no interest in Claire's friend. His eyes were glued to Claire as though he were in love all over again. Claire felt warm and tingly, regardless of whether she talked about Ben, her kids, or her love for photography.* What's going on here? Watch yourself Claire. I'm happily married. Well, I'm married, anyway.

- What is happening inside of Claire's brain at this point? Is this true love rediscovered or something else?

## 27. Why do we need to be emotionally cared for?

*The thing that I'm most worried about is just being alone without anybody to care for or someone who will care for me.*
—Anne Hathaway

- Why would Anne Hathaway, a stunningly beautiful, rich, famous actress make this statement? Is her wanting to be cared for healthy or unhealthy?

## 28. Why does the negative cycle kill connection?

Therapist: *Okay. So your communication has been dying over the years because you shut down or fight when you need each other the most. Claire, you have learned to keep your hurt to yourself as much as possible. Then Ben tries to talk to you and you explode with anger.*

- How does this cycle of communication kill relationships?

## 29. Why does sexual arousal change as relationships progress?

Therapist: *So, sexual intimacy came very naturally and you were highly aroused by each other. There were some mixed feelings on your part, Claire, but you had no doubt that Ben fulfilled you and you wanted to do the same for him. What happened in the years after you got married?*

- Why do you think Ben and Claire lost their originally satisfying sexual relationship?

## 30. How is new love idealization dangerous?

*After we are married, it's a different story: New love in that context can destroy our lives. The biological and spiritual purpose of new love is to ignite our rocket engines so we can defy the gravity that keeps us to ourselves. It inspires us to overcome our inhibitions and propels us toward the other person at the speed of light. It goads us into seductive behaviors such as flirting, sexual banter, and the overwhelming need for physical touch. These things can distract even the most committed people from their marriages. New love is full of big emotions—but it is also a predictable, biologically programmed drive. It has the power to destroy what we have spent a lifetime loving and sacrificing our lives for.*

- How does this interpretation of new love challenge the way that our culture idealizes it?

## 31. How does new love dopamine affect emotions and behavior?

*The novelty and intrigue associated with new and erotic relationships stimulates dopamine, the most powerful reward neurochemical known to man and beast.*

- How was dopamine affecting both Ben's emotions and behavior?

## 32. What is dating for attachment?

*Dating for dopamine, whether intentional or not, is about using another person as a mood-altering drug. When one is "addicted to love" while at the same time racing down the track into a lifelong relationship, the results can be disastrous. A marriage that comes from such a situation can be disastrous. When the excitement of new love inevitably wears off and the brain stops delivering mega doses of dopamine, it can be easy to question whether the relationship is the right fit after all. Casting it off and following the dopamine dating trail once again places us back in a vicious cycle. It won't be long before some new love object starts the intoxicating music again—perhaps this is the one? The results are all too predictable.*

- How does dating for attachment help us avoid the trap of dopamine-driven, addictive relationships?

## Part Five
## Adult Attachment: Love Left Behind
## and the Vital Science of Adult Attachment

## 33. How do we prioritize adult attachment?

*The weekend was nearing and Claire had to finish her work on the Chicago travel story. With the kids at school and Ben at work, she'd finally have some quiet time. Claire grabbed her laptop and began to polish what she had begun three weeks earlier. Her deadline wasn't going to flex because of Ben's affair. The hell with it . . .* I'm not going to let my problems with Ben ruin my career.

- What priority should career be given in an attached relationship?

## 34. Why do couples who love each other have affairs?

*Ben was doing all the talking. "There's something I still don't understand. This thing with Bridgette. I never intended it to happen. I mean, I wasn't looking for a relationship there. Even when Claire kind of shut down with me sexually, I wasn't looking for that from someone else. You see, that's just it—I wasn't looking for something else. I loved Claire."*

- Why do you think people who love their spouses have affairs?

## 35. Why are lovers' fights so dramatic?

*"Remember our wedding, Ben? When did we lose that magic? Was it all a big lie? Has our entire marriage been a farce?"*

*Ben's tone was rough now. "Claire, aren't you being a bit dramatic? 'A farce?' We had a plan and we're living it. Tell me, what have you wanted that you don't have? We've got our two beautiful kids. A gorgeous home in one of Chicago's finest suburbs. Did all that come from a lie, Claire? Your friends look at our life and see plenty of magic. Why can't you?"*

- What is happening here between Ben and Claire? Is Ben being too harsh? Is Claire in "la la land"?

## 36. What creates affair vulnerability?

*"Actually, yes. I have felt it for the last five years when everything and everyone in your life seemed more important than me. Yes, Claire. I've been studying and working my butt off trying to get licensed and get the practice up and running. For us. For our family. And you pretty much left me alone." A softness came over Ben. "So yes, I do know what it feels like."*

- Is this just an excuse that Ben is making up? Or had Ben and Claire's disconnection contributed to his vulnerability to having an affair?

## 37. Why is relationship betrayal often unintentional?

Ben: *I feel terrible. And I am afraid. I can't believe that this is happening to us either. I can't believe that we let ourselves grow so far apart and that I did this stupid thing! I never intended to betray Claire or destroy our relationship.*

- How often do you think that people who have no intention of having affairs fall victim to them?

## 38. Why do we withdraw in relationships?

Ben: *No, it wasn't. And, believe me, I knew that so very well from that moment, looking into your eyes. But in my urgency to undo the hurt I had caused you, I was desperate to make it smaller, walk it back, make it fade away. That was more about me, I know that now. I felt so ashamed about how I'd hurt you, I wanted just to sweep it under.*

- What does this say about how Ben handles emotional conflict?

- What happens to Ben when he tries to minimize the emotional injury?

### 39. Why do betrayers lie?

Claire: (Slowly nodding) *I mean, I feel he's lied to me so often, I don't know what to believe, but I hear this, and yes—*

- How do you explain how blatantly Ben lied to Claire?

### 40. How does mirroring create attachment?

*When children cry, mothers respond to see what is causing their distress. When children are happy and want to play, mothers are glad to smile back and join in the fun. This emotional mirroring and response to the need underlying the emotions is what forms the basis for secure attachment. Emotional mirroring and responsiveness to emotions is what makes human beings feel safe and cared for, whether we are one or ninety-nine years of age.*

- How were Ben and Claire failing to mirror each other's emotions?

- How do you think emotional mirroring forms the foundation for secure attachment?

### 41. How do emotions heal emotions?

*The denial of the importance of emotion decreases our ability to weather the emotional storms that come up in every close relationship. When we disconnect from our emotional warning-and-response system, we disarm our most important form of navigation to care for our partner and ourselves. Thinking and rational strategies are simply no match for emotional intelligence when it comes to making relationships work. Even bright and talented Ben could not strategize his way through the marital conflict he found himself in.*

- Why is it impossible to use reason alone to heal emotional injuries?

- How did the failure to recognize the importance of attachment emotions set Ben and Claire up for the trouble they were in and make their healing more difficult?

## Part Six
## Committed to Connection:
## Empty and Alone, Hope and Healing

### 42. How does knowing we are "first" heal and secure us?

*Ben told Claire about his concern that the new position would be even more consuming than his current one. He didn't want to upset the progress they were making, or make the circumstances that had led him to Bridgette even worse than they already were.*

*As they talked, Claire sensed that Ben was really torn about this—he wasn't just questioning his new opportunity for her sake; he was honestly saying that he felt he should be spending more time at home. More time with her. And yet, she knew he really wanted the job. "But. . . the job means a lot to you, doesn't it?"*

- How was Ben's change of heart about prioritizing Claire over career foundational in their healing?

### 43. Why do we need to need the love of another person?

*"Well, I'm starting to understand what the therapist has been saying about how I cling to you because I need the security you bring, your work and status. It's hard for me to admit it, but I can see some truth in it. And today, I think I understood something else. I think I need you for something else. I need you for just being there, being here, for me. Not the security of your image but the connection with you. I need you for this, Ben, what we're doing here, right now.*

- How was Claire's revelation critical to building a solid foundation in their love relationship?

## 44. How does sincerity heal relationships?

Claire: *I am swirling on the inside, too. This is such a change from the way Ben has related to me in the past. I do believe now that he is sincere. Though, it is going to take me some time to heal from everything that has happened.*

- How was Ben's sincere communication with Claire helping her to soften and begin to trust him again?

## 45. How do facial expressions reveal emotions?

Therapist: *Claire, what would it be like to turn toward Ben and to tell him that you want to trust him again and that you, too, need to find the connection you have lost? Is that something you think you can do?*

- Why do you think the therapist asked Claire to turn toward Ben and tell him that she wants to trust him and find connection with him?

## 46. Why must withdrawers learn to show emotion?

*When pursuers feel insecure, they express their emotions in an attempt to gain emotional reassurance from their partners. They want to know that their partner feels as deeply about an issue as they do. If their partner does not respond with emotional authenticity and accurately mirror their emotions, they become even more insecure. They try again, with even more emotional intensity, to get the point across. The expectation is that more emotion will surely pull at the heartstrings of their beloved. If the lack of emotional response persists, the pursuer often expresses attacking emotion and exasperation to try to get the withdrawer to engage. The conflict escalates.*

- Why is it so important for pursuers to see that withdrawers are feeling what they feel?

## 47. How do we escape the negative conflict cycle?

*This pursuer-withdrawer dynamic creates the perfect storm in nearly every troubled relationship. The pursuer's emotional flooding, or overload, causes the withdrawer to almost automatically flee rather than fight for the relationship. This pushes the primitive panic button in the pursuer. Pursuers must see their partner's emotion. They must know that their withdrawing partner cares emotionally about their deep pain. If this does not happen, the pursuit will continue on and on.*

- State in your own words how couples can learn to escape the damaging effects of a negative pursue withdrawal cycle?

## 48. How does shame interfere with relationship healing?

*Shame is a universal emotion that hinders our capacity to be transparent and to trust the emotional reaches of the one we love most. There is not a soul alive who does not struggle with feeling worthy of the unconditional love necessary to grow and thrive. Shame can be a self-defeating excuse for living outside of the experience of unearned love.*

- How do you see shame interfering with the healing of Ben and Claire's relationship?

## 49. How is grieving important for relationship healing?

*We also experience grief when there is an attachment violation or injury in the relationship. Wives often feel they can never restore the innocent trust that they once had in their husbands after the devastation of an affair. They need to be able to grieve, and grieving is not a one-time event. It comes in waves of emotion that must be expressed over and over again.*

- How can Ben and Claire help each other grieve?

## 50. How do needs and wants facilitate forgiveness?

*True emotional forgiveness in love relationships requires this heart-level exchange of needs and wants. It is simply too dangerous to forgive a lover who will not confess his or her deep emotional need for our love.*

- How can Ben continue to reassure Claire in a way that will allow her to trust him with her whole heart?

## 51. What does it mean to make your primary relationship primary?

*Making our primary primary in adult life is about giving our adult love relationships the priority and power to transform our lives. When we make our primary primary, we heal our past, present, and future. As we place our partner above any other human relationship, we protect and create safe space for our attachment bond to heal and transform our lives.*

- How were Ben and Claire taking their first steps to "make their primary primary"?

## 52. How do we strengthen emotional connection?

*Lunchtime passed pleasantly as they got to know the owners of the B&B, an older couple who seemed to love the life of hospitality. This became a welcome distraction for both Ben and Claire, each of whom was realizing desperately that they didn't really know how to navigate this time alone together, to do the work of true connection.*

- What are the three things Ben and Claire can do to strengthen their connection?

# Additional Resources
# for Emotional Connection

## Books for General Readers[*]

Johnson, S. (2008). *Hold Me Tight: Seven Conversations for a Lifetime of Love.* New York NY: Little Brown and Company, Hachette Book Group.

    In *Hold Me Tight,* Dr. Sue Johnson presents Emotionally Focused Therapy to the general public for the first time. Johnson teaches that the way to save and enrich a relationship is to reestablish safe emotional connection and preserve the attachment bond. Through case studies from her practice, illuminating advice, and practical exercises, couples can learn how to nurture their relationships and ensure a lifetime of love.

Johnson, S., Sanderfer, K. (2016). *Created for Connection: Hold Me Tight, Guide for Christian Couples, Seven Conversations for a Lifetime of Love.* New York NY: Little Brown and Company, Hachette Book Group.

    The message of *Created for Connection* is simple: Forget about learning how to argue better, analyzing your early childhood, or making grand romantic gestures. Instead, get to the emotional underpinnings of your relationship by recognizing that you are attached to and dependent on your partner in much the same way that a child is on a parent and we all are on the Heavenly

Father, for nurturing, soothing, and protection. The way to enhance or save our relationships with each other and with God is to be open, attuned, responsive, and to reestablish safe emotional connection.

Tatkin, S., Hendrix, H. (2016). *Wired for Dating: How Understanding Neurobiology and Attachment Style Can Help You Find Your Ideal Mate.* Oakland, CA: New Harbinger Publications.

This book offers simple, proven-effective principles drawn from neuroscience and attachment theory to help you find the perfect mate.

Tatkin, S., Hendrix, H. (2012). *Wired for Love: How Understanding Your Partner's Brain and Attachment Style Can Help You Defuse Conflict and Build a Secure Relationship.* Oakland, CA: New Harbinger Publications.

*Wired for Love* is a guide to understanding your partner's brain and enjoying a romantic relationship built on love and trust. Synthesizing research findings on how and why love lasts drawn from neuroscience, attachment theory, and emotion regulation, this book presents ten guiding principles that can improve any relationship.

Levine, A., Heller, R. (2010). *Attached: The New Science of Adult Attachment and How it Can Help You Find and Keep Love.* New York, NY: Penguin Group.

*Attached* guides readers in determining what attachment style they and their mate (or potential mates) follow. It also offers readers a wealth of advice on how to navigate their relationships more wisely given their attachment style and that of their partner. An insightful look at the science behind love, *Attached* offers readers a road map for building stronger, more fulfilling connections.

Siegel, D. J., Hartzell, M. (2013). *Parenting from the Inside Out: How a Deeper Self-Understanding Can Help You Raise Children Who Thrive*: 10th Anniversary Edition. New York, NY: Penguin Group.

Drawing on new findings in neurobiology and attachment research, the author explains how interpersonal relationships directly impact the development of the brain, and offers parents a step-by-step approach to forming a deeper understanding of their own life stories, which will help them raise compassionate and resilient children.

Goleman, Daniel. (1994). *Emotional Intelligence: Why It Can Matter More Than IQ*. New York, NY: Random House.

Everyone knows that a high IQ is no guarantee of success, happiness, or virtue, but until *Emotional Intelligence,* we could only guess why. Daniel Goleman's report from the frontiers of psychology and neuroscience offers new insight into our "two minds"—the rational and the emotional—and how they together shape our destiny.

Scazzero, P. (2006). *Emotionally Healthy Spirituality*. Nashville, Tennessee: Thomas Nelson.

In this best-selling book, Scazzero outlines his journey and the signs of emotionally unhealthy spirituality. Then he provides seven ways to break through to the life meant for you. "The combination of emotional health and contemplative spirituality that we might experientially know the power of an authentic life."

## Books for Therapists and Readers Who Want to Dig Deep[*]

Grossman, K. E., Grossmann, K., Waters, E. (Eds.). (2005). *Attachment from Intimacy to Adulthood: The Major Longitudinal Studies*. New York, NY, London: Guilford Press.

This volume provides firsthand accounts of the most important longitudinal studies of attachment. Presented are a range of research programs that have broadened our understanding of early close relationships and their role in individual adaptation throughout life. In addition to discussing the findings that emerged from each study, leading investigators offer rare reflections on the process of scientific discovery.

Fosha D., Siegel, D. J., Solomon, M.F. (Eds.). (2009). *The Healing Power of Emotion: Affective Neuroscience, Development, and Clinical Practice*. New York, NY, London: W. W. Norton & Company.

We are hardwired to connect with one another, and we connect through our emotions. Our brains, bodies, and minds are inseparable from the emotions that animate them. Normal human development relies on the cultivation of relationships with others to form and nurture the self-regulatory circuits that enable emotion to enrich, rather than enslave, our lives. And, just as emotionally traumatic events can tear apart the fabric of family and psyche, the emotions can become powerful catalysts for the transformations that are at the heart of the healing process.

Cozolino, L. (2006). *The Neuroscience of Human Relationships: Attachments and the Developing Social Brain*. New York, NY, London: W. W. Norton & Company.

Just as neurons communicate through mutual stimulation, brains strive to connect with one another. Louis Cozolino shows us how brains are highly social organisms. Balancing cogent explanation with instructive brain diagrams, he presents an atlas of sorts, illustrating how the architecture and development of brain systems from before birth through adulthood determine how we interact with others.

Karen, R. (1998). *Becoming Attached: First Relationships and How They Shape Our Capacity to Love.* New York, NY, Oxford: Oxford University Press.

In *Becoming Attached,* psychologist and noted journalist Robert Karen offers insight into some of the most fundamental questions of emotional life. Karen begins by tracing the history of attachment theory through the controversial work of John Bowlby, a British psychoanalyst, and Mary Ainsworth, an American developmental psychologist, who together launched a revolution in child psychology. Karen tells about their personal and professional struggles, their groundbreaking discoveries, and the recent flowering of attachment theory research in universities all over the world, making it one of the century's most enduring ideas in developmental psychology.

*All book descriptions are taken from Amazon.com

## Find an Emotionally Focused Therapist

Find an Emotionally Focused Therapist in your area: International Center for Excellence in Emotionally Focused Therapy.

# About the Authors

Authors Dr. Michael and Paula Regier are married and work together in the Center for Relational Excellence in Visalia, California. Michael earned his Ph.D. from the California School of Professional Psychology and has over thirty years of experience as a clinical psychologist. He is a certified Emotionally Focused Couples Therapist and Supervisor. He is a former faculty member at the Johns Hopkins School of Medicine in Baltimore, Maryland. He is currently an adjunct faculty member at the Kaweah Delta Psychiatric residency program in Visalia, California. Paula has a background in business and accounting. She has developed a second career as a neurofeedback technician where she helps emotionally over- and under-aroused individuals overcome trauma, find focus and achieve emotional balance. Michael and Paula are passionate about helping couples prevent relationship failure through attachment-based treatment and education. They have launched a Relationship Education Online Learning Course. Learn more about our online education at **RelationalU.com.**

Learn more at MichaelRegier.com.

# Notes

1   "AROUTIOUNIAN: The Price of Emotional Poverty." *Yale Daily News.* Accessed January 06, 2017. http://yaledailynews.com/blog/2013/10/07 /aroutiounian-the-price-of-emotional-poverty/.
2   Deraniyagala, Sonali. *Wave.* New York: Alfred A. Knopf, 2013, pp. 3–13.
3   Umassboston. "Still Face Experiment: Dr. Edward Tronick." *YouTube.* November 30, 2009. Accessed January 06, 2017. https://www.youtube. com/watch?v=apzXGEbZht0.
4   Picturealternatives. "Dads Try the Still Face Experiment." *YouTube.* April 26, 2016. Accessed January 06, 2017. https://www.youtube.com/ watch?v=6czxW4R9w2g&t=26s.
5   Schore, Allan N. *Affect Dysregulation and Disorders of the Self.* New York: W. W. Norton 2003.
6   Brown, Brené. "Listening to shame." Brené Brown: Listening to shame | TED Talk | TED.com. Accessed January 06, 2017. http://www.ted.com /talks/brene_brown_listening_to_shame.
7   Schore, Allan N. *Affect Dysregulation and Disorders of the Self.* New York: W. W. Norton 2003.
8   Watson, John B., and Rosalie Alberta (Rayner) Watson. *Psychological Care of Infant and Child.* New York: W. W. Norton & Company, Inc., 1928, pp. 81–82.
9   Spitz, Rene. *Psychoanalytic Study of the Child Vol. V11,* Madison, CT: International Universities Press, 1952.
10  Bowlby, John, and Margery Fry. *Child care and the growth of love. Abridged and ed. by Margery Fry. With two new chapters by Mary D. Salter Ainsworth.* Harmondsworth, Eng.: Penguin Books, 1965, p. v.
11  Goleman, Daniel. *Emotional Intelligence: Why It Can Matter More Than IQ.* New York: Bantam Books, 1995.
12  Erikson, Erik H. *Childhood and Society.* New York: Norton, 1964.
13  Fisher, Helen E. *Why We Love: the Nature and Chemistry of Romantic Love.* New York: H. Holt, 2004.

14  Hazan, C. and Shaver, P.R. (1987). Romantic love conceptualized as an attachment process. *Journal of Personality and Social Psychology, 52*(3), 511-524.

15  Coan, James A., Hillary S. Schaefer, and Richard J. Davidson. "Lending a Hand: Social Regulation of the Neural Response to Threat." *Psychological Science* 17, no. 12 (2006): 1032–039. doi:10.1111/j.1467-9280.2006.01832.x.

16  Coyne, James C., Michael J. Rohrbaugh, Varda Shoham, John S. Sonnega, John M. Nicklas, and James A. Cranford. "Prognostic importance of marital quality for survival of congestive heart failure." *American Journal of Cardiology* 88, no. 5 (2001): 526–29. doi:10.1016/s0002-9149(01)01731-3.

17  *ScienceDaily*. Accessed January 06, 2017. https://www.sciencedaily.com/releases/2000/12/001214160933.htm.

18  Hawkley, Louise C., and John T. Cacioppo. "Loneliness Matters: A Theoretical and Empirical Review of Consequences and Mechanisms." *Annals of Behavioral Medicine* 40, no. 2 (2010): 218–27. doi:10.1007/s12160-010-9210-8.

19  Kiecolt-Glaser, Janice K., Timothy J. Loving, Jeffrey R. Stowell, William B. Malarkey, Stanley Lemeshow, Stephanie L. Dickinson, and Ronald Glaser. "Hostile Marital Interactions, Proinflammatory Cytokine Production, and Wound Healing." *Archives of General Psychiatry* 62, no. 12 (2005): 1377. doi:10.1001/archpsyc.62.12.1377.

20  Simpson, J. A. (1990). Influence of Attachment Styles on Romantic Relationships. *Journal of Personality and Social Psychology, 59*(5), 971-980.

21  Mikulincer, Mario, and Phillip R. Shaver. *Attachment in Adulthood: Structure, Dynamics, and Change.* New York: Guilford Press, 2007.

22  Fenney, Brook. *J Posit Psychol.* Author manuscript; available in PMC 2016 Mar 17. Published in final edited form as: *J Posit Psychol.* 2016; 11(3): 246–257. Published online 2015 May 29. doi: 10.1080/17439760.2015.1048815. PMCID: PMC4795838. NIHMSID: NIHMS699331

23  Johnson, Susan M., and Leslie S. Greenberg. "Emotionally Focused Couples Therapy: An Outcome Study*." *Journal of Marital and Family Therapy* 11, no. 3 (1985): 313–17. doi:10.1111/j.1752-0606.1985.tb00624.x.

Made in the USA
San Bernardino, CA
11 February 2020